Stefan Buczacki

Best Container Plants

HAMLYN

Publishing Director Laura Bamford
Design Manager Bryan Dunn
Designer TT Designs
Executive Editor Julian Brown
Editor Karen O'Grady
Production Clare Smedley
Picture Research Jenny Faithfull

First published in Great Britain in 1996
by Hamlyn a division of Octopus Publishing Group Limited
Michelin House, 81 Fulham Road, London SW3 6RB

Produced by Toppan Printing Co.(HK) Ltd.
Printed in Hong Kong

ISBN 0 600 59748 2

A catalogue of this book is available at the British Library

CONTENTS

INTRODUCTION 4

BENEFITS AND CONSTRAINTS 5

TYPES OF CONTAINER 6

COMPOSTS 10

PLANTING 11

CARE OF CONTAINER PLANTS 13

USING CONTAINERS IN THE GARDEN 14

PLANT DIRECTORY

ANNUALS 18

TENDER PERENNIALS 44

HARDY PERENNIALS 52

BULBS 60

ROSES 69

SHRUBS 71

TREES 80

DWARF CONIFERS 86

HERBS 90

INDEX 94

INTRODUCTION

This is a very difficult book to write, because, as I have remarked on many occasions, I believe that any plant can be grown in a container. It is simply of matter of finding the right container and putting it in the right place. By that token, this could have been an encyclopaedia of the plant kingdom. It isn't, of course, because of the limitations of space and my energy. I therefore lay emphasis on the 'Best' of the title. The plants I include are those that have performed best for me in outdoor containers and have given me particular pleasure. So although you will find in these pages most of the types that are commonly container-grown, you will find many unexpected ones, too, for I want you to share the satisfaction I gained from succeeding with them and, even more importantly, I want to encourage you to experiment.

People have grown plants in containers for as long as they have gardened and pictures of plants in containers (if not the real thing) can be seen among the ruins of ancient civilizations. But the variety of containers has never been greater than it is today. Containers come in an enormous range of sizes, shapes, style and materials. There are containers to suit every garden and every purse, containers that are purely and unashamedly functional and containers that are truly and magnificently beautiful. On pages 6–9, I outline some of the main types and the considerations to bear in mind when choosing them. For simplicity, however, I give a broader indication of the containers I have found most suitable for each type of plant in the Directory entries. The categories I use there, and my definitions of them are:

Hanging basket Includes any container that is freely suspended at some distance above the ground and has the limitations imposed by free drainage.

Window box Any more or less oblong-shaped, box-style container designed to fit on to a windowsill, although as I describe on page 9, the plants may be grown in separate containers within the main box.

Small tub Any free-standing tub, of whatever shape, up to a diameter and height of about 20cm (8in). The category includes containers of this size raised on a pedestal.

Large tub Any free-standing tub, of whatever shape, greater in height and diameter than about 20cm (8in).

There are a few rather special types of container available such as growing bags and ring-culture pots that are used for growing tomatoes and similar crops and these are described on page 9.

You can in fact extrapolate most of what I say about container gardening to the growing of plants in any very tiny, confined situation, although as will become apparent, containers have the special difficulty associated with no access to soil moisture.

Fuchsias and helichrysums blend well in a hanging basket

Window boxes with trailing plants

BENEFITS AND CONSTRAINTS

Although container-gardening is centuries old, it is, if you think about it, an uncommonly odd way of going about things. After all, plants do not naturally grow in containers and I can only assume that container-gardening came about originally because of our ancestors' desire to subjugate the plant kingdom, to confine it and bend it to their will. Growing plants in containers could never be performed on a large enough scale to replace the growing of plants in the open ground, but having invented it, ancient man must have discovered that container-gardening has both advantages and disadvantages – with many of the latter being beyond their wit or resources to counter.

BENEFITS

Containers can be positioned more or less where you wish: you do not need to find an appropriate area of open soil. Sites in the garden that otherwise would be dull and unproductive can be brightened and used to good purpose. Most importantly, if you have no open garden soil or no garden at all, you can still enjoy the pleasure and satisfaction of growing plants. Moreover, you can position the containers where conditions are optimal for your chosen plants: those that suffer from exposure can be tucked safely out of the wind; those that suffer from direct sun can be put in dappled shade. And containers can be moved (unless they are very large) which offers several benefits. You can take them to the greenhouse, potting shed or wherever else is convenient for planting up, free from the limiting factors of the weather. They can even be put at a convenient working level on a potting bench. And mobility means that you can place a container in its display position when the plants are at their most attractive and move it away again, or even dispose of it entirely, once that time is over.

Gardening in a container allows you to grow plants that are wholly unsuited to the type of soil occurring naturally in your garden. By selecting an appropriate compost (see page 10), you can grow acid-loving plants in an alkaline district, or plants that need a free-draining sandy loam even if your garden soil is better suited to making plates!

By and large, the plants in your containers should be untroubled by weeds and the majority of the soil-inhabiting pests and diseases that occur in an open garden. That said, some problems like wine weevil have made the container environment very much their own.

CONSTRAINTS

Of course, container-gardening has some distinct disadvantages. First, it is essential to use a specially formulated compost, because almost all types of garden soil simply do not behave as required in a container. They lose their structure and become no better than thick pudding.

The choice of compost type is most important and I consider it in detail on page 10. Whichever compost you choose, its nutrient content is finite. Even in the real soil of a real garden, where plants' roots are continually exploring new areas, supplementary feeding becomes necessary sooner or later. In a container, this happens even sooner than it does in the open soil. But perhaps the biggest constraint of all on container-gardening is watering. Unable to tap into any moisture reserves, plants that are neglected in a container will die of water shortage very quickly; and of course, a hanging basket, with its almost unrestricted drainage, creates the most ridiculous situation of all. Regular attention to watering, either manually or by some automated system is essential. I consider the various watering and feeding options on page 13.

Hydrangea **in a fairly shaded spot**

Pansies in a hanging basket

TYPES OF CONTAINER

A visit to any garden centre will reveal a huge array of containers, varying in size and shape and manufactured from a wide range of materials. Aesthetic considerations and cost will play a major part in dictating which containers to choose; in general plastic is the cheapest, the least attractive and functionally it has perhaps the greatest drawbacks. However, there are certain features that are important when containers are used for any individual purpose. On these pages I look at some of the factors you should take into account when making your choice.

One of the secrets of good container planting is to achieve a balance between foliage and flower interest

FREE-STANDING CONTAINERS

A cubic metre (1 cubic yard) of potting compost weighs approximately 1 tonne (1 ton). So, if you plan to move full containers around, the size of the container and the volume of compost it holds are important. I find that a terracotta tub about 40cm (16in) tall and 35cm (14in) in diameter is the maximum I can move comfortably when full (concrete containers of the same size will of course be heavier). Bear in mind that portability isn't everything: many superficially attractive containers contain too small a volume of compost to be functionally effective. These containers fail partly because they require watering unrealistically often and partly because there is insufficient space for the roots of any plant with large enough leaf and flower growth to be attractive. Some concrete containers, for instance, appear fairly large on the outside but have very thick walls and a very limited internal space, perhaps shaped like an inverted pyramid. (Some of the containers sold for attaching to walls likewise possess very small internal volumes; I discuss the special situation of hanging baskets on page 9 but flat-backed wall pots are in my experience particularly troublesome.) As a general rule of thumb, I advise against choosing any container that has an internal volume less than that of a conventional 15cm (6in) diameter plant pot.

Stability is another important factor to consider. In practice it is a function of several features: height, the ratio of height to diameter, volume of compost, type of compost (soil-based composts are much denser than peat-based ones), size of plant, and relative exposure and windiness of the site. Again, I can only advise according to my own experience, but I suggest that you try to avoid those containers which taper sharply, where the basal diameter is less than about two-thirds of the top diameter. The taller the container, the more important this ratio becomes.

MATERIALS

Plastic I would never for preference choose a plastic container: they always *look* like plastic containers (and thus inferior); they are easily damaged if moved when full; many types discolour and become brittle with age; and plastic containers have the considerable drawback of being impermeable to water and air. Thus plants in them are likely to suffer from waterlogging which will almost undoubtedly lead to root damage. But plastic containers do have the advantage of being relatively cheap so if you are taking over a new garden, you

can purchase a large number to give the garden immediate colour at a time when there will certainly be more pressing demands on your funds. If you must begin your container-gardening career with plastic pots (or even with really make-do vessels such as old paint cans), I suggest you gradually replace them, one or two per year, with more attractive and traditional types.

Terracotta The unglazed earthenware called terracotta has been used to make plant containers for centuries and

Small 'feet' improve drainage

Tulip 'Spring Green' in pot

How much better a weathered old pot looks than a brand new one

is undeniably lovely, if expensive. But choose carefully. There are some very attractive imported pots that cannot tolerate even a slight degree of frost without flaking or cracking and so must be taken under cover in the winter. The frost-tolerance of terracotta depends on the nature of the clay used and the way that it is fired. Some British manufacturers are now so confident of their materials that they offer a ten-year frost-resistance guarantee so you can safely plant these pots with perennials and leave them outdoors permanently. But for efficiency, use your non-hardy terracotta pots for plants such as specimen fuchsias that must themselves be taken into the protection of a greenhouse or conservatory in the winter.

Stone Containers hewn from natural stone are beautiful but they are now extremely difficult to find and prohibitively expensive. Their place has been taken by moulded concrete and reconstituted stone vessels, some of which are so well made it is difficult to distinguish them from the real thing. Check that these containers, too, are frost-tolerant and that they do not contain any chemical setting or hardening agent that might, until the pot is really well weathered, be toxic to the plants inside it. The easiest way to encourage the external growth of lichen and algae to simulate more closely the appearance of a genuine old stone container is to paint the concrete occasionally with milk or liquid cow manure.

Half-barrels In theory, a container for permanent planting can be as big as you choose but once you move into the realm of pots larger than about 60–75cm (24–30in) in diameter, you are beginning to talk big money. The best value, among really big containers, are undoubtedly wooden half-barrels, although you must select carefully: choose real half-barrels, not made-up items as the latter will be nowhere near as durable. The maximum lifespan I have obtained from a half-barrel container is about ten years, and this is likely only if you line the container with plastic sheet (with holes for drainage), in order to keep the compost and the wood from coming into contact. Don't forget that, as with all containers, half-barrels should be raised on small 'feet' or pebbles to improve drainage, help limit freezing damage and keep out crawling pests. And remember to drill several drainage holes in the barrel itself before you fill it with compost. It is very difficult to move a half-barrel when it is full. If you have to, try using three rollers cut from lengths of old scaffolding pipe; few other readily available materials are sufficiently strong.

For large container plantings, half-barrels are probably the best value

OTHER CONTAINERS

Window boxes These are a special delight in inner-city gardens, provided they are out of reach of vandals, and for apartment dwellers. Much the best system is to invest in wooden boxes (which may have to be made specially) of the same size and shape as your window ledge, with drainage holes. The boxes should be treated with preservative inside and lined with plastic sheet. You can then place plastic troughs and pots containing the plants within this wooden frame. This arrangement allows you to plant up the containers (and even let the plants mature) before you place them on the window ledge in view; and it also gives you the flexibility of replacing individual pots or troughs during the summer.

Hanging baskets They are very appealing but hanging baskets can present a number of special difficulties too. Their weight when full and wet is a major consideration: you must ensure that support brackets are strongly anchored. Many modern baskets are too shallow to be effective and the compost inevitably dries out very rapidly – a basket should preferably be at least 30cm (12in) in diameter and at least 18cm (7in) deep.

Growing-bags Although a popular form of container, growing-bags have serious limitations. In the greenhouse, I much prefer the ring-culture system of raising tomatoes and similar plants and I urge all greenhouse tomato growers to consider it very seriously. However, growing-bags are certainly useful for cultivating tomatoes, cucumbers and similar crops outdoors on paved areas where there is no access to bare soil. There are now several ways of over-

Window boxes can be used for plants differing as widely as small-flowered narcissi, ivies and small shrubs

coming the difficulty of providing support for plants raised in this way.

The plastic growing-bag has a major drawback: watering is exceptionally hard to regulate since it is impossible to see if the compost is wet or dry and plants can easily end up suffering from one or other of these extremes. Certainly the growing-bag is no system for anyone who is likely ever to be away from home for several days at a time, unless they wish to invest in an automated watering system (see page 13).

Trough containing an attractive blend of lobelia and *Begonia semperflorens*

COMPOSTS

Garden soil in a container is not a satisfactory growing medium, and so gardeners these days turn to artificial composts. Such preparations are nothing new, of course; for many years every commercial nurseryman and grower, and to some extent, every amateur gardener too, had his or her own jealously protected formula for blending soil with manure, leaf-mould, fertilizers and other ingredients to produce an enduring structure in which to grow their plants.

SOIL-BASED COMPOSTS

In the past, an individual making a small amount of compost could ensure that it was more or less uniform, but it was not possible on a large, commercial scale. All this changed with the studies made during the 1930s at the John Innes Horticultural Institute, England. These led to the development of the John Innes Seedling and Potting Composts and laid down the standards to which gardeners in Britain still adhere today. The novel features of this range were: the use of steam-sterilized loam of defined type; the use of peat instead of manures and composts; the accurate dosing of fertilizers; and the discovery that a small range of potting composts could serve for a wide range of plants.

Because of the types of fertilizer employed, the original John Innes composts had to be used very quickly after preparation. Modern commercial versions of this compost have a much longer shelf-life, although you should nevertheless buy fresh each season.

Currently, there are four John Innes composts on the market: a Seedling formula and numbers 1, 2 and 3 Potting formulae. By and large, the higher the number, the greater the fertilizer content and thus the longer plants will grow in it satisfactorily. No 1 is most appropriately used for the first potting-on of young plants raised in the Seedling mixture; No 2 is ideal for plants grown for one season; and No 3 is for the long-term growing of perennials.

Recently, a number of branded composts called simply John Innes Potting Compost have appeared. As far as I can see, these approximate to John Innes No 2 and shouldn't therefore be used for trees, shrubs or other long-term plants. All John Innes composts will require supplementary fertilizer in due course (see page 13).

SOIL-FREE COMPOSTS

After World War Two, the increasing shortage of high-quality loam and the rising costs of transportation led to the development of alternative seedling and potting composts. The most important for gardeners have been those based on peat, both the highly acidic moss or sphagnum peat, and the less acidic sedge peat. The biggest differences between these composts and soil-based ones are that they offer an even greater uniformity in commercial production; and they are light and easier to handle. Against these benefits must be set the fact that peat is devoid of natural nutrients. This means that once the added fertilizer is exhausted, there is no reserve on which the plants can draw and so supplementary feeding must begin far sooner.

Every gardener should be aware of the need to conserve the rich wildlife habitats that comprise many bogs and moors from which peat is dug. This is not to suggest that peat should not be used in the garden; rather that its use should be kept to a minimum and the only brands you should buy are those stating they originated in areas that are not of scientific importance.

Because of the swing in opinion in recent years over the use of peat, a number of other materials have been appraised; coir, derived from waste coconut husk, has been one of the more important. Unfortunately, all alternatives so far investigated suffer from one drawback or another, usually concerning the retention of nutrients and/or moisture. There has therefore been a significant shift of favour back to John Innes composts. I for one have all but abandoned soil-free composts, except for two purposes. I use them in hanging baskets (where a lighter compost is more practical and nutrient-retention is of short-term importance), and also in the container-growing of plants that need a highly acidic medium. For these, peat-based composts have no serious challengers as yet.

Iris and *Choisya* **will thrive better in a soil-based compost**

PLANTING

Putting a plant in a container is, in essence, no different from planting it in the open garden. If, like rhododendrons, they should be planted shallowly in a border, then they should be planted at this soil level in containers, too. And if a small tree requires a stake for support in the garden, likewise it should be staked in its tub. For container-gardening, however, it is in the timing of planting and the arrangement of the plants within the containers that you should take extra care.

Some types of container are filled first with compost and then planted, while others are filled piecemeal as the plants themselves are put in position. Hanging baskets, parsley (or strawberry) pots and, by and large, any containers with bulbs should be filled piecemeal. But before you put any plants into a container that has already been filled with compost, do be sure you haven't *over-* filled it. You must allow for the volume taken up by the plants' roots and, if you have pot-raised them, by the compost in which they are already growing. Also it is important to ensure that when the whole assembly is complete the upper-surface of the compost remains about 3–4cm (1–1½in) below the rim of the container; otherwise, it will be washed out when the plants are watered.

When planting a hanging basket, be sure that fast-growing foliage plants won't obscure the small flowers of less vigorous types

HANGING BASKETS

Despite being such a common and familiar garden feature, these are in reality not easy to plant well. It's important to select a good lining material that will serve the dual purpose of helping conserve moisture and retaining the compost, so that it doesn't fall through the holes. (As you will gather from my remarks on page 9, I am not enthusiastic about hanging baskets of anything other than the conventional basket form.)

The best lining material is sphagnum moss but you should never pull it up from its natural habitat: if you can't obtain it from garden centres or other suppliers, you should choose other natural plant- or animal-based materials; some excellent wool-based materials are now available. You may find various solid and durable liners on sale but I find these quite useless as they offer far too little drainage.

After lining the basket, place a small volume of compost in the base of the basket and feed any trailing plants carefully through from the inside. As with all planting into containers with holes, you will usually damage the plants if you attempt to push them through from the outside. Gradually fill the container with more compost, topping up as you put each layer of plants in place. Once the basket is about three-quarters full of compost, position the top plants, starting with one large specimen plant at the centre.

Position plants such as *Thunbergia* (which will climb upwards) close to the supporting chains of the basket while planting genuine trailing types, like cascade forms of lobelia and nepeta, at the edges.

Gardeners are spoiled for choice in plants for summer containers

STRAWBERRY POTS

Strawberry pots and parsley pots are filled along much the same lines as hanging baskets. Put compost in the bottom of the pot up to the level of the first holes; carefully push the plants through from the inside and then add more compost up to the next layer of holes; and so on up to the top. Don't be tempted to use small or weaker plants at the sides of the pot: this is the position most likely to suffer if watering and feeding are neglected. Put your best plants closest to the bottom of the pot.

TUBS

With tubs and other types of container that are pre-filled with compost, follow the usual maxim with regard to plant size: put one or more large plants in the centre of the tub, then work outwards using progressively smaller and less vig-orous ones (remember it is *ultimate* size that matters), and finish with trailing plants at the edge.

WINDOW BOXES

The most obvious way to plant a win-dow box is to treat it much like any other pre-filled container (making sure, if it is wooden, you line it first with plas-tic sheet in which a few drainage holes have been made). However, this isn't necessarily the best and certainly not the most versatile way to use a window box. As described on page 9, it is much better to grow each plant in its own individual pot and place these in the box, packing around and under the pots with a soil-free compost. In this way, you can easily move and replace indi-vidual plants if they deteriorate, with-out disturbing the box as a whole.

SUMMER PLANTS

Always remember that most summer container plants are half-hardy and so must be kept under protection and then hardened-off before you plant them outside. In the case of a hanging basket, this generally means that you should plant up the basket as a whole and keep it under protection for sev-eral weeks, so do make sure that you have some suitable place, for example a cool greenhouse, where this can be done. If you leave planting up the basket until after the last frosts, you will have few flowers until late in the season.

WINTER PLANTS

It is important to remember that when planting winter containers of all types, especially hanging baskets, plants grow very little during the winter months. So don't put in small plants and expect them to fill out the basket; they won't. Use big plants and completely fill the container with them. You should also bear in mind that winter-flowering plants, winter pansies especially, really should be in flower when they are planted. To plant a rosette of leaves in autumn and expect it to produce masses of flowers over the succeeding six months really is asking a great deal.

BULBS

To obtain a long period of colour when using bulbs in large containers, select bulb varieties of different flowering times. If you use species that have dif-ferent bulb sizes, bear in mind that the bulbs must then be layered: the larger types must be planted more deeply than the smaller ones. The easiest way to do this is again to fill the container piecemeal: put in compost to the depth required for the largest bulbs, place the bulbs in position, add more compost up to the next planting depth, and so on. The smallest types, such as crocuses, can simply be pushed in from the sur-face of the filled container.

You will have to use more foliage for winter plantings

CARE OF CONTAINER PLANTS

Because all container plants will be grown in an artificial potting compost, in which (as I noted on page 10) the nutrient content is finite, supplementary feeding is essential for healthy growth.

SUMMER ORNAMENTAL ANNUALS AND TENDER PERENNIALS

These plants grow rapidly during their relatively short lifespan and should be fed with a water-soluble or liquid fertilizer that can be absorbed quickly. With a soil-free compost, feeding should begin approximately six weeks after planting; with a soil-based compost, feeding can begin after about eight weeks. The type of fertilizer that you use isn't critical but a brand that contains rather more potash in relation to the nitrogen and phosphate is ideal, since this encourages the development of flowers at the expense of foliage. You should feed the plants once a week.

SUMMER VEGETABLE CROPS

Similar treatments are needed for summer vegetable crops, although a more balanced fertilizer, with proportionately more nitrogen, is preferable for leafy plants such as lettuces. Tomatoes and other greenhouse container crops need more nurturing. Like summer ornamentals, they should be fed with a high-potash product. Special 'tomato' formulations are preferable: these generally contain various trace elements to prevent leaf-yellowing and to encourage the best fruit development. These greenhouse crops should be fed once a week from the time the first fruits have set, although many gardeners find that, in warm summers, feeding twice a week is necessary.

FOLIAR FEEDING

Foliar feeding is exactly what the term suggests: the application of liquid fertilizer to the leaves rather than to the roots of the plants. The method can certainly be beneficial during times of very rapid growth but you should appreciate that plants can absorb considerably less nutrient through their leaves than through their roots.

My policy is to apply the fertilizer to the compost but I don't prevent it splashing onto the leaves as well, so that I have the best of both worlds.

LONG-TERM PLANTS

Long-term container plants being grown in a John Innes No 3 Potting compost are best fed in much the same way as smaller plants growing in the open soil: with a balanced general fertilizer such as fish, blood and bone, if they are foliage types, with a supplement of sulphate of potash in the early spring for fruiting species.

WATERING AND MULCHING

Just as the nutrient in a container is finite, so is the water supply. All annuals in containers should therefore be watered at least twice a week, and hanging baskets should be watered daily. You can achieve a small 'buffer' against neglect by incorporating a proprietary water-retaining gel with the compost of hanging baskets, and also by covering the compost surface with a layer of granules to limit water lost through evaporation. If you must be away from home for days at a time, your best bet might be to install a trickle-watering system, connected either to the mains or a reservoir tank.

Long-term container plants in large tubs should always be well mulched in the early spring, just as if they were in the open garden. This helps maintain the compost in a moist condition through the summer.

DEADHEADING AND PRUNING

Deadheading, the removal of spent flower heads during the flowering season, is very important in maintaining both the appearance and performance of annuals in containers. The dead flower heads are very likely to attract diseases; moreover, the removal of them can encourage the development and breaking of new flower buds, and thus prolong the flowering season.

Long-term woody perennials may also require pruning if they are to give of their best over a period of years. They require the minimum pruning once established, but for the first few years after planting it is important to build up a framework of sturdy branches, removing weak, crossing and misplaced shoots in the dormant season so that a symmetrical and balanced plant results.

REPOTTING

Although gardeners don't seem quite as obsessed about repotting outdoor container plants as they are about house plants, the subject does crop up frequently. Annuals remain in the same containers for the duration, so the subject doesn't arise; and I discuss the situation with bulbs on page 60. For other perennials, notably trees and shrubs, it is hard to give overall guidelines but it is unlikely that even the faster-growing container shrubs will require repotting more than once every four or five years. I have had a number of slow-growing container shrubs and trees that have remained in their pots for many years.

USING CONTAINERS IN THE GARDEN

The value of containers in the garden is two-fold: firstly, they produce something that is instantly appealing; and, secondly, as far as long-term planting is concerned, they can be used to complement other features of the garden, either blending with them relatively unobtrusively, or becoming major features in their own right. Indeed, in a small garden, or in a small courtyard within a larger garden, a container plant can be almost the sole component of note.

We need at the outset to distinguish between temporary and permanent plantings. The most significant among the more obvious differences concerns size. Few short-term containers are very large precisely because few short-term plants are very large. By contrast, most long-term containers and plants are pretty big (the only really important exception, as regards plant size at least,

being alpines). The consequence of this is not just a matter of visual impact, however, for permanently planted containers, being big, tend to be jolly heavy. They are therefore likely to stay put – with the comparitively rare exceptions of containers holding tender perennials, which by some means or another must be rolled under cover in the autumn. The wonderful potted citrus

trees so beloved of eighteenth-century orangery owners are the classic examples of this practice, but really you should avoid emulating it unless there is truly no likelihood of giving yourself a serious medical problem.

Your choice of containers for permanent plantings will almost certainly be dictated ultimately by cost but I urge you to buy the best and most attractive that you can afford. To my mind, there is absolutely no point in creating some long-term feature in your garden if you have had to compromise on its appearance. Aesthetics aside, the only really important criterion is that the material must be durable, and I suppose that the ultimate material (although for most gardeners, the *unattainable* ultimate) is lead. But I would place good-quality terracotta a close second.

GARDEN DESIGN

It is worth giving some thought to how containers can fit into your garden as a whole, and how they can fulfil a specific

Lead containers are the ultimate, in appearance and cost

A heavy terracotta pot is a permanent feature in this garden design

and clearly defined purpose. First, let's examine how the use of a container can enable you to do things in terms of garden design that otherwise you couldn't.

Hard areas These are both a blessing and a curse: paving, gravel, stone chippings and other physically hard surfaces can make the difference between being able to walk from place to place easily in winter, and your lawn turning into a quagmire. In addition, they present a neat way of making small gardens, or small areas in large gardens, attractive and relatively maintenance-free all year round. But hard areas don't offer you the flexibility of bare soil; you can't simply put plants where you wish and it would be silly to smash holes hither and thither to create planting positions. Here containers come to the rescue compensating for the versatility hard areas lack – for they do indeed mean that a choice plant can be put just where you wish. Thus you can instantly create a focal point in a paved courtyard, or a feature that will brighten up a dark corner. Nowhere is this facility so much appreciated as against a wall; here, by using a container, a climber can clothe a surface that otherwise would be bare.

In a paved area container-plantings can make a very attractive small self-contained garden

Pots of pelargoniums at the edge of steps help to break the formal line

Use your very best plants and containers to frame your front door

CONTAINERS AS GARDEN LANDSCAPE

I want now to look in rather more detail at the contribution that containers can make to the overall design of the garden by providing important structural features. In general, a major contribution will be made by a single large container, although it's a mistake to think that this must invariably be so, and the use of containers on steps is a classic example why not. Use small pots, even standard 15cm (6in) plant pots, filled with a range of trailing or other plants; position them one at either end of each step and you soften the hard lines, producing something that will positively encourage people to walk up the steps and discover other parts of your garden.

We aren't all blessed with gardens that have changing levels. My own garden is naturally flat but I have countered this deficiency by using containers and there is no reason why you should not do the same. Use a large, tall container to give the illusion of height in an otherwise flat area of garden; the feature will also draw the eye, either towards some other equally-interesting feature beyond, or perhaps away from some less attractive part of your plot. Do try to select something in harmony with the rest of the garden; evidently rustic or informal containers will never look right as the central feature of a formal, regimented area.

There can be no better feature in any formal garden than a well-sculpted piece of topiary, and there is every reason to grow your topiary in a container. The geometric shapes, balls, pyramids and pillars, have a special appeal when standing in a finely turned terracotta pot.

The front door The front of your house is immensely important as it immediately conveys to your visitors a good deal about you and your home. If you have limited resources, and can afford only one or two really choice containers, you might choose to position them either side of the front door. Depending on the plants they contain, you can convey an impression of structured formality or casual *laissez-faire*.

CONTAINER CROPS

It's a mistake to think that containers can only add to the ornamental appeal of your garden. There's no reason why they can't contribute to the production of fruit and vegetables, too, as long as you don't aspire to self-sufficiency.

Among the vegetables, so many different types can be grown in containers that it's easier to pick out those few that are not appropriate for container-growing. I wouldn't bother with most brassicas, especially the really big ones such as Brussels sprouts; and I'd be loath to spend much effort on sweetcorn or globe artichokes, again for reasons of size. But everything else will work well, including potatoes in large buckets or dustbins – indeed, a bin of potatoes in a cool greenhouse is a wonderful way of obtaining the very earliest

crop. And container-grown vegetables can look attractive, too: the feathery foliage of carrots, the rich red leaves of beetroot and, yes, the flowers of potatoes. All in all, it is a very satisfying way of growing vegetables.

Furthermore, if you intersperse your vegetables with pots of herbs like thyme, sage or mint, the versatility, usefulness and attractiveness of your container-garden is further enhanced. Every variety of herb just cries out to be cultivated in a container and, of course, parsley has even given its name to a special type of pot with holes in the sides.

Fruits, too, make excellent container plants especially since, unlike vegetables, with fruit you really can approach self-sufficiency. Fruit trees, especially apples on dwarfing rootstocks, are ideal for growing in containers; if you

choose a 'family' apple tree, with two or three varieties grafted on to the same stock, you can have apples for every purpose.

For some strange reason, soft fruits (with the obvious exception of strawberries) tend to have been grown rather less frequently in containers; perhaps it's the rather untidy spreading nature of raspberries and currants that puts people off. However, even such thirsty plants as grapevines can be grown very successfully in containers, provided you ensure the containers are really deep and you pay special attention to watering.

This all goes to reinforce what I find myself saying time and time again. Any plant can be grown in a pot; it's simply a matter of the right person finding the right pot.

Small vegetables in a trough

A delightful selection of container-grown thymes

ANNUALS

Annuals, plants grown each year from seed, occupy the largest section of this book. This is, as much as anything, a reflection of the fact that, for most people, containers are for summer. Although in many cases, it's perfectly possible to sow the seed directly into its growing position, this isn't in practice the best method. The reason is that, in a container, every plant must count; there's no room for uneven germination and growth. In any event, half-hardy annuals can't be safely put outside until after the danger of the last frost is over. Therefore, if raising your own plants, much the best method is to sow the seed in individual modules in the greenhouse or cold-frame. You can then select the best plants to go in the prime spots within your containers.

Ageratum (HHA)

❝ *Ageratums have acquired the unfortunate and unflattering name of floss flowers and, indeed, they do have a look of candy floss about them. They are among the very best of compact powdery blue annuals although there are also some pink- and white-flowered forms that I would rather leave in* the catalogues. *The only drawback is that the flowers die rather untidily, although this is much more evident with the whites. All are derived from the Mexican species (*A. houstonianum*), but they vary in size and, for container planting, the taller, 'cut-flower' types are much less valuable.* ❞

SPECIAL FEATURES
Sow seeds in late spring on surface of the compost and keep it moist to encourage growth and flowering.

SUITABLE CONTAINERS
Window boxes and large tubs.
HEIGHT Varies with variety, usually from about 15cm (6in) to 60cm (24in).

RECOMMENDED VARIETIES
All of the following are relatively compact, reaching 15–20cm (6–8in): 'Adriatic' (F₁), mid-blue; 'Blue Danube' (F₁), lavender blue; 'Capri', deep blue.

Ageratum 'Capri'

Alyssum (Lobularia) (HA)

❝ *Common and easy it may be, but I still consider the Mediterranean alyssum (now more correctly called* Lobularia maritima*) to be the best white cushion-forming annual (although other colours exist too). In my garden it self-seeds among the paving slabs where the previous season's containers have stood. When the time comes to weed out the excess plants, you will appreciate its common name, sweet alyssum, for the crushed leaves exude a delicious aroma. This is all the more reason for growing it closer to eye and nose level so that it can be appreciated.* ❞

SPECIAL FEATURES
Mildew prone in hot summers so it is better if grown in a cooler position and very light shade.

SUITABLE CONTAINERS
Window boxes and large tubs.
HEIGHT 10cm (4in) to about 25cm (10in); seeds of supposedly the same variety can vary widely.

RECOMMENDED VARIETIES
White flowered: 'Carpet of Snow' ('Snow Carpet'), but try to obtain a 'selected' or 'improved' strain; 'Little Dorrit'; 'Snowdrift'.
Red flowered: 'Wonderland' (also called 'Wonderland Red').
Purple flowered: 'Oriental Night'; 'Royal Carpet'.
The mixtures are best avoided.

Anchusa (HA/HB)

" I don't know why more seed companies don't offer anchusas for they have an intensity of blue matched by little else, except perhaps for the best lobelias. Like lobelias, their wild parent, A. capensis, is South African. In form they resemble their relatives, the forget-me-nots, but do be sure you obtain the compact variety (see next column). "

SPECIAL FEATURES

Best treated as an annual for flowering later in the summer but can also be sown in the autumn as a biennial for blooming in the spring. It needs to be grown in a sunny position.

SUITABLE CONTAINERS
Window boxes, small and large tubs.
HEIGHT 20–25cm (8–10in).

RECOMMENDED VARIETIES
'Blue Angel' is the only really suitable form; it is frost hardy and can be treated as a biennial. 'Dawn' is a mixture with white, pinks and mauve shades but with nothing else particularly special to commend it. 'Blue Bird' is considerably taller and not really suitable for growing in a container, while others, such as 'Royal Blue', derived from A. azurea, are taller still.

Anchusa 'Blue Angel'

Aster (*Callistephus*) (HHA)

" The asters I am concerned with here are derived from the oriental plant known as Callistephus chinensis. They have suffered a decline in popularity in recent years, due as much as anything to a mysterious wilt disease (see next column), although I think the tide is now turning again in their favour. In the past, I have been as guilty as many another gardener of neglecting the lower growing or 'bedding' forms which make splendid container plants, offering a considerable range both in colour and in the shagginess of their flowers. In containers, of course, with fresh compost each year, aster wilt provides no fears. "

SPECIAL FEATURES

Aster wilt results in feeble plants when asters are grown for several years on the same soil. Some varieties have resistance but this is irrelevant for container growing.

RECOMMENDED VARIETIES
Several of the varieties have simple descriptive names such as 'Blue Bedder', 'Pink Bedder' and 'White Bedder', but a particularly good single-coloured form is 'Blue Skies'. There are also many good mixtures including 'Dwarf Comet', 'Milady Mixed', 'Chrysanthemum Flowered Mixed' and, for masses of smaller flowers, 'Pinocchio'.

Aster 'Milady Mixed'

SUITABLE CONTAINERS
Larger window boxes, small and large tubs.
HEIGHT Bedding varieties range from 15cm (6in) to 25cm (10in).

Begonia (HHA/TP)

" For the container garden, there are three main groups of begonias: the tuberous varieties, generally kept as perennials from year to year (see page 44), the fibrous-rooted forms derived from the Brazilian species B. semperflorens *and raised annually from seed, and an intermediate group, the 'Non-Stop' varieties which produce tubers but tend to be raised afresh from seed each year. It is the fibrous-rooted begonias that are the most valuable in containers with their neat, compact habit, their lush, glossy foliage, their bright, positive flower colours and their very reasonable shade tolerance. I can't imagine container gardening without them. "*

B. semperflorens 'Olympian White'

SPECIAL FEATURES

Fibrous-rooted begonias have tiny seeds but the seed companies have devised various ways of overcoming the difficulty. As with all small seeds, however, they should be sown on the surface of the compost. Allow six months from sowing to flowering time.

SUITABLE CONTAINERS

Window boxes, small tubs, large tubs, hanging baskets.
HEIGHT 15–30cm (6–12in).

RECOMMENDED VARIETIES

Fibrous-rooted varieties: among the best of the New F_1 hybrid varieties is the 'Olympia' series, which offers a rich red with deep bronze foliage, white with fresh green foliage, pink with light-green foliage and 'Starlet' with bicoloured white and pink flowers. Among others that have given me good results are the 'Thousand Wonders' range, with red-, pink- and white-flowered types, but there are also many different mixtures, each seed company having their own blends. Check the descriptions carefully as the pale green-leaved plants produce a very different effect from the dark bronze-foliaged types.

Tuberous-rooted varieties: the 'Non-Stop' F_1 hybrid mixtures offer large double flowers in a wide range of colours including orange, pink, red, yellow, apricot and white.

Bellis (HB/HP)

" Generally, I don't find biennials useful as container plants as they occupy the space for a long time before producing any flowers. But I make an exception for Bellis *daisies. I have included them partly because they are perennial, although grown as biennials, but mainly on the grounds that they are small and can be grown in individual pots ready for planting out at an early stage. "*

SPECIAL FEATURES

Sow the seed in early summer to obtain flowers by the following spring.

SUITABLE CONTAINERS

Small pots, window boxes.
HEIGHT 10–20cm (4–8in)

RECOMMENDED VARIETIES

Unfortunately most seed companies only offer mixtures. However, single colours – red, pink or white – are obtainable; look out especially for the 'Carpet' range.

Bellis perennis

Brachyscome (HHA)

" The Australian Swan River daisy is a plant that I took to some years ago and no-one can be more delighted than me that the full range of single colours has once again become available. They have the perfect combination of feathery foliage and tiny, star-like flowers, for once, not tainted with any double forms. Take note and be warned: single is beautiful. So pretty and reliable are they that they are gradually taking over the places in my containers formerly occupied by lobelias. "

Brachyscome 'Blue Star'

SPECIAL FEATURES

Don't sow brachyscomes too soon as they grow quickly and, especially if they aren't pinched back, you will have very straggly plants by the time they can be planted out (after the frosts are over).

SUITABLE CONTAINERS

Small pots, hanging baskets, window boxes. I have found small terracotta pots very effective.
HEIGHT 25–30cm (10–12in).

RECOMMENDED VARIETIES

'Blue Star', 'White Splendour' and 'Purple Splendour' are obtainable together with a mixture of all three; the purple form is much the finest.

Browallia (HHA/TP)

" I rather expect browallias to be among the next batch of plants to enjoy a burst of popularity as well as the serious interest of plant breeders. Today, they are most likely to be seen as house or cool greenhouse plants but in reasonably warm summers, they make wonderful hanging basket subjects too. Like so many another half-hardy summer garden flowers, they come from South America and, as close inspection of their slightly trumpet-shaped flowers will reveal, they belong to the potato family. "

SPECIAL FEATURES

The best way to raise browallias for outdoor, summer containers is to sow them at the same time as pelargoniums, fibrous-rooted begonias and other slow-growing, small-seeded species to produce plants large enough for planting out. For indoor winter-flowering plants, sow again during the summer.

SUITABLE CONTAINERS

Hanging baskets, window boxes.
HEIGHT Usually from about 20cm (8in) to 25cm (10in).

Browallia 'Blue Troll'

RECOMMENDED VARIETIES

'Blue Troll', deep blue; 'White Troll'; 'Blue Bells', rich blue flowers with long trumpets and trailing stems, too.

Calceolaria (HHA/TP)

❝ I have said publicly on many occasions that I can't stand calceolarias, but my real dislike is for the large-flowered pot varieties. For good strong yellow colour in bedding plants, the smaller forms take some beating. I do know that many gardeners don't share my opinions and all calceolarias are very popular plants. The bedding types for containers are hybrids derived from one or more South American species and they are difficult to categorize, as some are strictly tender perennials, while others are more or less hardy biennials. In practice, all tend to be grown as half-hardy annuals. ❞

SPECIAL FEATURES
Sow the minute seeds on the surface of the compost. Do not allow it to dry out.

Soft, silver *Senecio* foliage softens the impact of bright *Calceolaria*

SUITABLE CONTAINERS
Window boxes, small and large tubs, hanging baskets.
HEIGHT 15–20cm (6–8in).

RECOMMENDED VARIETIES
'Sunshine' (F_1), the best golden yellow strain; 'Midas' (F_1), golden yellow; 'Sunset' or 'Sunset Mixed' (F_1), a mixture of red and yellow bicolours, rather more vulgar; there are also other mixtures including the rather taller 'Little Sweeties Mixed', but there are so many colours in these mixtures, it is impossible to plan your planting accurately.

Calendula (HA)

❝ What a lovely, lovely old garden flower this is, the southern European edible pot marigold, with a freshness of orange that is almost unmatched. I grow calendula all over my kitchen garden where they contrast so beautifully with the green of the salad vegetables. I also grow them in pots and dot these among the vegetable beds, only moving them out when the vegetables start growing large enough to threaten them. Yes, whether they are the taller varieties in the open soil or the dwarf forms in containers, calendulas are among the indispensible plants of my summer. No garden should be without them. ❞

SPECIAL FEATURES
Flower best in conditions of low nutrient, so grow them on their own or with nasturtiums (see page 42) in pots of soil-based seedling, not potting, compost. May need spraying against mildew.

SUITABLE CONTAINERS
Small and large tubs.
HEIGHT 25–30cm (10–12in).

RECOMMENDED VARIETIES
'Fiesta Gitana', a mixture of orange, tangerine and yellow. Separate colours may sometimes be seen as 'Yellow Gitana' and 'Orange Gitana'.

Few colours can match *calendulas*

Campanula (HHA/HP)

Campanulas, the bellflowers, are a large and very diverse group of flowers, the most important of which are border perennials and rock garden species. In recent years, however, they have made a stunning impact on the container-gardening scene with new varieties of a small trailing species from Northern Italy called Campanula isophylla. *There is little else quite like it and once you have mastered the art of handling its very tiny seeds, you will be enchanted.*

SPECIAL FEATURES

As with most tiny-seeded plants, it is essential to sow them early; about six months is required from sowing to flowering, even with good, warm greenhouse conditions.

SUITABLE CONTAINERS

Hanging baskets, window boxes, small and large tubs.
HEIGHT Usually reach between 20cm (8in) and 30cm (12in).

RECOMMENDED VARIETIES

There are three varieties you are most likely to see: 'Kristal Blue', 'Kristal White' (sometimes a mixture of these two may be offered but this seems quite pointless to me), and a rather more compact form called 'Stella'. This latter form also exists in blue and white and is sometimes very usefully sold as a twin-pack of seeds, one of each colour, rather than the two mixed together.

Campanula isophylla **'Kristal Hybrids'**

Cerastium (HA/HP)

Cerastium tomentosum, snow-in-summer, from mountainous regions of Europe and Asia, is a proper Jekyll-and-Hyde plant. It looks sweet and innocent and, indeed, is very pretty with its masses of tiny white flowers and silvery foliage, but it will spread and self-seed with such wicked abandon that I certainly wouldn't plant it in the open garden. In containers, however, it is relatively easy to show it who is in charge, and it is a valuable plant for supplying both the white and the silver-grey to a planting.

SPECIAL FEATURES

In containers, cerastium fares better in seedling rather than potting compost.

SUITABLE CONTAINERS

Small and large tubs.
HEIGHT 15cm (6in).

RECOMMENDED VARIETIES

Usually the normal species will be all that is offered. A better choice, as it bears more flowers, is the selected form var. *columnae* 'Silver Carpet' or 'Silberteppich'.

Cerastium tomentosum

Chrysanthemum (HA)

" *If the name* Cineraria *(right) is confusing, it can't hold a candle to* Chrysanthemum, *a genus that has been rent asunder and then reassembled in recent times. The group that I'm concerned with here is perhaps the least known although for several years it did comprise the entire genus. These are the annual chrysanthemums, so valuable for summer containers and embracing five species of which* C.coronarium *is the most valuable although for convenience, I've also included a few other worthy annuals.* "

SPECIAL FEATURES

The taller types must be pinched back as they then branch readily to form a neat bushy habit. Many varieties contain an attractive blend of single, double and semi-double flowers.

SUITABLE CONTAINERS

Window boxes, small and large tubs, hanging baskets (depending on variety and habit).
HEIGHT Varies with species from about 15cm (6in) to 45cm (18in).

RECOMMENDED VARIETIES

Varieties of *Chrysanthemum coronarium* 'Golden Gem', golden yellow; 'Primrose Gem', mid-yellow, superb, the best of the annual chrysanthemums. Varieties of *C. multicaule* (syn. *Coleostephus myconis*): 'Gold Plate', golden yellow, neat habit; 'Moonlight', lemon yellow, neat habit, an excellent hanging-basket plant. *C. paludosum* (syn. *Leucanthemum paludosum*), daisy flowers with white rays and yellow centre – excellent in small tubs.

Chrysanthemum **'Golden Gem'**

Cineraria *(Senecio)* (HHA/TS)

" *The name cineraria means different things to different people. Perhaps it most immediately brings to mind an image of the bright, daisy-like house plant widely sold by florists. This plant has flitted around the genera and has now come to rest as* Pericallis x hybrida *but it doesn't make a good outdoor container plant. The plant sold as* Cineraria maritima *(although now more correctly called* Senecio cineraria*) does. It's a Mediterranean, silver-foliaged species and, although naturally a big shrub, it is one of the few foliage container plants you can raise as an annual from seed.* "

SPECIAL FEATURES

You should take great care to avoid damping-off after the seeds have germinated because the soft, felty leaves attract moisture like a sponge. Don't expect flowers; there won't be any.

SUITABLE CONTAINERS

Window boxes, small and large tubs, hanging baskets.
HEIGHT Varies from about 20cm (8in) to 30cm (12in).

RECOMMENDED VARIETIES

'Silver Dust', fern-like leaves, compact ('Dwarf Silver' seems the same to me); 'Cirrhus', more rounded, less divided leaves and better moisture tolerance.

Cineraria maritima

Coleus *(Solenostemon)* (HHA/TP)

❝ *Coleus tend to be thought of today as easy-to-grow house plants with a range of beautiful foliage colours. However, they also have value as outdoor container plants wherever a dazzling display of leaf colour is required. They aren't easy to blend with other plants; to capitalize on their appearance, select plants with the best colours for future seasons. Coleus do produce flowers but they are rather uninteresting and I pinch them out. As with so many other garden plants, the old name has been declared redundant and coleus now belong to the genus* Solenostemon. *Still, it is as* Coleus *that you will invariably find them listed.* ❞

SUITABLE CONTAINERS
Window boxes, small and large tubs, hanging baskets.
HEIGHT 20–45cm (8–18in).

RECOMMENDED VARIETIES
It doesn't really matter which seed mixture you use to start planting in containers. However, you will find that the 'Wizard' and 'Fairway' ranges tend to be lower growing and are therefore of most value for container gardening. Some ranges have been specially selected for their cascading branches which makes them particularly attractive in hanging baskets; the most widely available of these is the aptly named 'Scarlet Poncho'.

SPECIAL FEATURES
The best plan is to raise the plants from seed in one year, pinching them back to create bushy specimens. Select your favourite colours and then take softwood cuttings, overwintering them in the greenhouse to provide a stock of uniform and predictable plants for future seasons.

Coleus offers the richest of velvets

Convolvulus mauritanicus

Convolvulus (HHA)

❝ *Yes,* Convolvulus *is the bindweed, and yes, it is a perennial that all of our gardens could do without. But it has some extremely attractive and trouble-free relatives that add their delightful trumpet-like flowers to container displays during the summer. Even these so-called bushy forms have something of a trailing habit which makes them especially useful for hanging baskets. Choose your varieties carefully and don't be tempted to try the very vigorous true climbers, either of* Convolvulus, *or of the closely related tropical genus* Ipomoea, *the morning glories.* ❞

SPECIAL FEATURES
Be careful in your choice of colours; there are some glorious deep blues and purples with white or pale centres, but some selections have extremely lurid multicoloured flowers.

SUITABLE CONTAINERS
Window boxes, hanging baskets.
HEIGHT 30cm (12in).

RECOMMENDED VARIETIES
Large-flowered varieties of *C. tricolor*: 'Rainbow Flash', pinks, reds and purples with pale centres; 'Ensign Blue'; 'Ensign White'; 'Ensign Rose'; 'Royal Ensign', blue with white centre and yellow eye. *C. mauretanicus* (syn. *C. sabatius*), smaller, variable pink to pale blue with slightly yellowish centres.

Coreopsis (HHA)

❝ There are so many lovely golden daisies for the summer garden that it always saddens me how few of them work really well in containers, generally because they are simply too tall and don't respond well to being pinched back. Fortunately, coreopsis aren't among them and I've grown them successfully in tubs for many years but it is important to remember that they need full sun. Most summer daisies from the southern hemisphere, like these, will disappoint in any shade; or, indeed, in dull summers over which you have less control. ❞

SPECIAL FEATURES
Don't confuse the annual species with the tall herbaceous perennials, much in evidence in garden centres.

Coreopsis tinctoria

SUITABLE CONTAINERS
Small and large tubs.
HEIGHT 30cm (12in) to 35cm (14in) for dwarf types; 45cm (18in) for taller types that should be pinched back; some are taller still and are not satisfactory.

RECOMMENDED VARIETIES
Varieties of *Coreopsis basalis*: 'Golden Crown', rich golden yellow with dark red centres; 'Early Sunrise', golden yellow, double. Low-growing selections of *C. tinctoria* are sometimes sold as 'Dwarf Mixture'.

Cuphea (HHA/TS)

❝ There will always be some plant genera that never receive the recognition they deserve, yet, when they are grown, they invariably prompt interested questions. Cuphea, from South and Central America, is just such a genus and two species in particular are wonderful when grown as half-hardy annuals for hanging baskets. ❞

SUITABLE CONTAINERS
Hanging baskets, window boxes.
HEIGHT 25cm (10in) to 30cm (12in) as an annual.

SPECIAL FEATURES
Cuphea grow best in sunny situations, but must be kept moist. After use in the summer, the plants, or cuttings from them, may be potted up and used as excellent house plants. Alternatively, retain them in order to take further cuttings in spring for outdoor use.

RECOMMENDED VARIETIES
Cuphea ignea (cigar flower), masses of tiny tubular orange-red flowers with black tips; *C. hyssopifolia* (false heather), tiny tubular flowers in mauve, pink or white.

Cuphea ignea

Dianthus (HA)

❝ *Everyone knows the genus* Dianthus, *which includes carnations, pinks and, less expectedly, Sweet Williams. But sadly, 'buttonhole' florists' carnations aren't easy to grow (they really need a greenhouse), while pinks are short-lived perennials that soon look straggly. If you turn to your seed catalogue you will find a delightful (if sometimes slightly vulgar) array of annuals derived from* D. chinensis *(often called* D. heddewigii*). I find that separate varieties grown in containers without the clutter of other plants work best. Some perennial types of* Dianthus *can be raised from seed; some are recommended as summer bedding and could be grown in containers. I find they flower rather too late in the summer to give full value.* ❞

SUITABLE CONTAINERS
Small tubs, hanging baskets, window boxes.
HEIGHT 15–30cm (6in–12in).

SPECIAL FEATURES
I never pinch back *Dianthus* as they respond by becoming unsightly and twiggy but it is important to snip off the dead heads regularly.

Dianthus **'Strawberry Parfait'**

RECOMMENDED VARIETIES
All of the following are single unless stated otherwise: 'Baby Doll', white, pinks and red; 'Black and White Minstrels', double, white and dark purple bicolour, very strange; 'Colour Magician' (F₁), flowers begin white but change through pink to almost red as the flowers mature; 'Fire Carpet' (F₁), vivid crimson; 'Frosty Mixed', double, frilly flowers (reminiscent of old laced pinks) in a range of bicolours and tricolours; 'Princess' (F₁), white, pinks, mauves, red; 'Raspberry Parfait' (F₁); 'Snowfire' (F₁), white with scarlet centres, pretty frightful; 'Strawberry Parfait' (F₁); 'Telstar' (F₁), mixture which includes some lovely colours and some terrible bicolours; 'Mixed Doubles', most of the colours.

Diascia (HHA/TP)

❝ *It was relatively late in my horticultural career that I encountered* Diascia *and since then I have never let them go. They have relatively long, trailing spikes of almost shell-like flowers in a limited range of pink shades. Today not all seed companies stock them or, alternatively, they have the annoying habit of dropping them for a few years without warning. They are derived from the South African* D. barberae, *are certainly sun-loving and they are nearly hardy in dry areas.* ❞

SPECIAL FEATURES
Despite their South African origin and need for sun, they must have some shelter from intense heat. For this reason, I have found that they make excellent plants for a mixed planting in big hanging baskets, when the larger plants around them will afford protection. Although it can sometimes be difficult in these situations, diascias will benefit from being trimmed back hard after flowering in order to prolong their flowering period. You must ensure that you keep them well watered.

SUITABLE CONTAINERS
Hanging baskets, window boxes.
HEIGHT 25–35cm (10–14in).

RECOMMENDED VARIETIES
'Pink Queen', mid-pink with deeper pink centres; 'Rose Queen', rose pink; 'Ruby Field', rose pink.

Eccremocarpus (HHA/TP)

❝ *There aren't many good annual climbers restrained enough to use in containers, but the Glory Vine is one that has worked well for me. It has an exotic feel with its tubular flowers in reds, orange and yellows, and these are complemented by the ferny foliage. By pinching it out two or three times, it is possible to produce a plant compact enough for use in hanging baskets but I have also found it successful when grown on wigwam supports in large tubs.* ❞

SPECIAL FEATURES

As it is really a perennial, it can easily be perpetuated by cuttings taken from overwintered stock plants in early spring and this is the way to obtain single colours, for only the orange-flowered species will come true; other seed-raised plants will be a mixture.

SUITABLE CONTAINERS

Large tubs, hanging baskets.
HEIGHT 2m (6½ft) to 3m (10ft) but, with repeated pinching back, can be restricted to about 1m (3ft).

RECOMMENDED VARIETIES

The true species *E. scaber* has orange flowers. The various mixtures, 'Anglia Hybrids', 'Fireworks', 'Carnival Time', 'Tresco Hybrids' and 'Mardi Gras Mixed' contain yellow, red and pink. From these, you can make selections for cuttings.

Erigeron (HA/HP)

❝ *Erigeron is another of those big genera of daisies (around 200 species in this instance) where it is important to use the correct species in your containers; some of the large border perennials would be a serious embarrassment. The correct one here is a plant that will be familiar to anyone who has had the pleasure of visiting some of the gardens designed by Gertrude Jekyll, in particular Hestercombe in the West of England. There the Mexican Erigeron karvinskianus has self-seeded into the stone walls with charming abandon, where it grows as a perennial, but by sowing early, you can treat it like any other annual when its classically simple daisy flowers on wiry stems will delight you all summer.* ❞

SPECIAL FEATURES

Once you have grown it, even in a container, you will almost certainly find self-sown seedlings cropping up in cracks and crevices but it will never become out of hand.

SUITABLE CONTAINERS

Small tubs, large tubs, hanging baskets.
HEIGHT 20–30cm (8–12in).

RECOMMENDED VARIETIES

The true species with its little white- and pink-rayed and yellow-centred daisy flowers will be found in plant nurseries; seed catalogues seem to call it 'Profusion' but I'm sure there's no difference.

Eccremocarpus scaber

Erigeron karvinskianus

Gazania (HHA/TP)

" *Gazanias belong to a group of South African daisies known in their homeland as 'civil servant flowers'; they can be seen in the morning but go to sleep in the afternoon. In reality, going to sleep, or closing their flowers, follows the clouding of the sky and can happen at any time of day. Knowing the unpredictability of the British summer, it might be thought that any plant that folds up at the onset of cloud is a pretty unreliable bet, but crafty work by plant breeders has resulted in varieties that stay open for longer.* "

SPECIAL FEATURES
Single colours can be perpetuated by selecting plants and taking cuttings in early spring.

SUITABLE CONTAINERS
Small tubs, large tubs, window boxes.
HEIGHT 20–30cm (8–12in)

RECOMMENDED VARIETIES
'Talent' (which has tended to replace the similar mixture called 'Carnival'), silvery foliage, flowers in deep and pale pink, yellow, cream and bronze; 'Chansonette', 'Harlequin' and 'Sunshine', all mixtures with varying proportions of several pinks, orange, yellow and cream although selections are now offered called 'Chansonette Pink Shades' and 'Chansonette Bronze Shades' which have a more limited colour range; 'Daybreak', a mixture with a rather darker central eye; 'Mini-Star' range, which has smaller flowers, available as mixtures of pinks, yellow, cream-white and orange or, uniquely, as 'Mini-Star White', which is the only pure white gazania; 'Orange Surprise', a particularly neat, 15cm (6in) high, variety with stunning flowers of the hot fiery orange that the true species displays in the grasslands of South Africa.

Gazania 'Daybreak'

Briza maxima

Grasses (HA)

" *Grasses play an important part in my ornamental plantings and look effective growing through gravel and stone chippings, but most of these are perennials. My container plantings are mainly of annual grasses, and 10 or more annual species are now commonly available from most seed catalogues, although it is important to choose carefully as they are not all equally effective and I would always steer clear of mixtures.* "

SPECIAL FEATURES
My experience is that ornamental grasses don't mix very well with other types of annual, at least not in the same container, and they look very much better when grown as single species.

SUITABLE CONTAINERS
Small tubs, large tubs.
HEIGHT Varies with species from about 30cm (12in) to 60cm (24in); because of their light, graceful habit, you can use fairly tall grasses in containers.

RECOMMENDED VARIETIES
Briza maxima and *B. media* (quaking grasses), nodding cone-like flower heads on slender stems that rustle in the breeze; *Hordeum jubatum* (squirrel tail grass), very feathery, more-or-less nodding flower heads of shiny green-brown; *Lagurus ovatus* (hare's tail), soft, silky, upright, white flower heads; effective.

Heliotropium (HHA)

❝ The bedding heliotrope, or cherry pie, was one of the favourites of the Victorian garden, partly for its rich, deep purple flowers and green-purple foliage but also for its fine fragrance. In former times, heliotropes were invariably raised from cuttings, but there are now a few seed-raised varieties, one of which is particularly valuable for containers. ❞

SPECIAL FEATURES

They are most effective when planted with small-flowered yellow species. I saw a very effective planting of heliotrope with the yellow canary creeper (see page 42) in a stone tub.

Heliotrope 'Marina Purple Splendour'

SUITABLE CONTAINERS

Large tubs, small tubs.
HEIGHT 30–35cm (12–14in).

RECOMMENDED VARIETIES

'Mini Marine' (syn. 'Dwarf Marine').

Impatiens Busy Lizzie (HHA/TP)

❝ The busy lizzie derives from the East African Impatiens walleriana and includes flowers in white, red, pink and orange. I have mixed feelings about them for they embrace some of the colours that I love least but they do tolerate more shade than any other bright-flowering annual. With the more recent advent of the New Guinea hybrids, we have the added dimension of truly striking foliage. ❞

SPECIAL FEATURES

Raising busy lizzies from seed isn't easy. Allow a period of six months from sowing to flowering, sow the small seeds sparingly, barely covering them with compost, incubate at around 22°C (71°F) and ensure good ventilation after germination to avoid damping-off.

Impatiens 'Blitz'

SUITABLE CONTAINERS

Window boxes, hanging baskets, small tubs, large tubs.
HEIGHT 10–35cm (4–14in).

RECOMMENDED VARIETIES

Of the main groups, almost all are F_1 hybrids. The following are the best that I have tried:

Group 1: large flowers on fairly tall plants, 30–35cm (12–14in); 'Blitz Orange', 'Blitz Mixed'.

Group 2: smaller flowers and a more compact habit, 15–20cm (6–8in); 'Accent' series in at least seven single colours and mixtures; 'Super Elfin Mixed', over 11 different colours (supposedly) – some available as individually coloured 'Elfin' varieties and there are some picotee forms in the range; the 'Tempo' series of at least seven individual colours and a mixture.

Group 3: various forms with double flowers; 'Confection Mixed'; 'Rosette Mixed'; some companies now claim that the plants in these mixtures will all have either double or semi-double flowers but in my experience most strains still give rise to some singles.

Group 4: the 'New Guinea Hybrids', 'Tango', tangerine flowers and dark green-bronze leaves; the 'Spectra' range of at least five single colours and a mixture are among the most recent of the gradually increasing number of New Guinea hybrids which can be raised successfully from seed.

Lathyrus Sweet pea (HA)

❝ There is no finer summer-flowering annual than the sweet pea but until very recently, I wouldn't have recommended it as a suitable plant for growing in a container. Even in a large tub with a wigwam support, the familiar Spencer varieties are just too large, but there is now a most appealing range of low-growing types. ❞

SPECIAL FEATURES

The flowers should be deadheaded to ensure continuity of new blooms. To raise them from seed, I sow them in pots in the greenhouse in early spring, transfer the young plants promptly to the cold-frame and then plant out.

SUITABLE CONTAINERS
Dwarfs: window boxes, hanging baskets, small tubs.
Intermediates: small/large tubs.
HEIGHT Varies between the lower-growing groups; the true dwarfs will barely reach 30cm (12in); the intermediates, about 1m (3ft).

RECOMMENDED VARIETIES
Unless stated otherwise, all include most of the full colour range of red, pink, mauve, blue and white.
Dwarfs (all mixtures): 'Bijou'; 'Cupid', white, pink, red and mauve bicolours; 'Little Sweetheart'; 'Patio'; 'Snoopea'.
Intermediates: 'Continental', 'Explorer', 'Jet-Set'.

Lobelia (HA)

❝ I have recently fallen out with lobelias as they have let me down in a way that I cannot quite understand. The blues have for many years been the mainstay of small-flowered trailing and clump-forming container plants that it has come as a surprise to discover that they burn so easily in hot weather and are finished before the summer is half over. I haven't dispensed with them completely, and nor should you, but be aware of their need for constant moisture and a spot out of the most fierce sun. ❞

SPECIAL FEATURES

Always sow the tiny seeds on the surface of the compost and in small clumps. Some varieties are sold as pelleted seed to make handling easier although greater care must be taken with germination conditions and they must not be allowed to dry out. Note also that all white-flowered lobelias will include a small number of blue-flowered plants.

Sweet pea 'Patio Mixed'

Lobelia 'Riviera Lilac'

RECOMMENDED VARIETIES
Compact varieties: 'Rapid Blue' and 'Rapid White' are quicker growing and flowering; 'Cambridge Blue', pale blue; 'Crystal Palace' and 'Crystal Palace Compacta', dark blue, bronze foliage; 'Mrs Clibran', dark blue, white eye; 'Riviera Lilac'; 'Riviera Blue Splash', white, pale blue and dark blue, strikingly different; 'Rosamund', red, white eye; 'Snowball', white; 'White Lady'; mixtures such as 'String of Pearls'.
Trailing varieties: 'Sapphire', dark blue, white eye; 'Blue Cascade'; 'Red Cascade'; 'Ruby Cascade'; 'Regatta Marine', dark blue, white eye, striking green foliage; 'Fountain' series.

SUITABLE CONTAINERS
Compact varieties: window boxes, small tubs, large tubs.
Trailing varieties: hanging baskets, window boxes, small tubs, large tubs.
HEIGHT 15cm (6in) for compact varieties; 25–30cm (10–12in) for trailing varieties.

Matricaria 'Snow Dwarf'

Matricaria (HHA)

“ Among the many annual small-flowered daisies, I always think that matricarias are the ones that most immediately remind you that they are in the same family as chrysanthemums. Many of my garden visitors think so, too, and imagine that these little double flowers are actually baby florists' chrysanthemums. An especially appealing feature is the ring of slightly larger outer florets on each flower. The colour range is limited but this is no bad thing. Matricarias are among those annuals that I like to see given containers to themselves, for maximum impact. ”

SPECIAL FEATURES
The tips should be pinched two or three times to encourage the attractive chrysanthemum-like bushy habit.

SUITABLE CONTAINERS
Large tubs, small tubs.
HEIGHT 15–25cm (6–10in).

RECOMMENDED VARIETIES
'Butterball', pale yellow with white outer florets; 'Golden Ball', uniform rich yellow; 'Lemon Santana', mid-yellow; 'Snow Dwarf', white with yellow centres.

Matthiola (HHA)

“ Allow me to introduce one of the most confusing groups of all plants you can raise from seed, the stocks, with a name that covers rather a large range of dissimilar, although related, plants. They are most familiar as richly perfumed cut flowers, and not everyone would think of growing them in containers. I do and most work magnificently. The annuals are divided into 'Ten Week' stocks, which flower ten weeks after sowing, the 'Trysomic Seven Week' stocks, which flower after seven weeks, and 'Beauty of Nice' types, which flower later than the ten-week types. The biennials are divided into 'Brompton' stocks and the 'East Lothian' stocks. ”

SPECIAL FEATURES
The ideal in stock growing is to obtain all double flowers. The ways to achieve this are strange in the extreme. With 'Ten Week' and 'Brompton' stocks, choose 'selectable' varieties and reduce the temperature to about 7°C (45°F) after germination. The potentially double-flowered plants then develop pale yellowish leaves. With 'Seven Week' stocks, the stronger seedlings produce the double flowers. With 'Stockpot', choose those seedlings with a small notch in their seed leaves.

SUITABLE CONTAINERS
Large tubs, small tubs.
HEIGHT 20–60cm (8–24in). All can and should be pinched back.

Matthiola 'Brompton Stock'

RECOMMENDED VARIETIES
Apart from 'Stockpot', there are few unambiguous individual variety names so simply choose mixtures of the groups that appeal to you, remembering to choose 'selectable' strains where appropriate.

Mimulus (HHA)

❝ *I don't like mimulus; so what are they doing among my best container plants? It is quite simply that I can recognize a plant that does its job well even though, personally, I find the combination of flower form and colours unattractive. For their many devotees, however, they are certainly cheerful plants. Bear in mind that their wild relatives are species of the bog side and river bank; they won't tolerate drying out.* **❞**

SPECIAL FEATURES

If they must be planted in full sun, then be sure the compost never dries out. Remember, they are among the very few shade-tolerant annual flowers; placing them in a slightly shaded spot will brighten a dull corner and ensure they are less likely to dry out. Mimulus have the advantage of requiring only two months from sowing to flowering.

SUITABLE CONTAINERS
Hanging baskets, small tubs, window boxes.
HEIGHT 15–30cm (6–12in).

RECOMMENDED VARIETIES
All F₁ hybrids; 'Calypso', yellow, orange, deep red and pink, including some bicolours; 'Magic', white, cream, yellow, orange, pink and red with some white and cream bicolours; 'Malibu', cream, orange, yellow and red; 'Malibu Orange', single-coloured, very striking.

Nemesia (HHA)

❝ *I was told recently that there is a greater variety of colours in nemesias than in any other summer-flowering annual. But this can cause problems as the mixtures are amazingly difficult to blend with anything else. All bedding nemesias are derived from the South African N. strumosa but they have the same drawback as lobelias, in that they are intolerant of very hot, dry conditions. Keep them well watered with space to grow.* **❞**

SPECIAL FEATURES

As container plants, nemesias sometimes fail to please because their flowering season is relatively short. The trick is to sow them successively in small tubs or in small pots and pop them into window boxes, replacing each old batch as it fades.

SUITABLE CONTAINERS
Small tubs, window boxes, hanging baskets, large tubs.
HEIGHT 20–25cm (8–10in).

Mimulus 'Malibu' series

Nemesia 'Carnival'

RECOMMENDED VARIETIES
Single colours: 'Blue Gem', charming mid-blue with white eye; 'KLM', blue and white bicolour – the colours of the Dutch national airline; 'Mello White'; 'National Ensign', violent red and white bicolour; 'Orange Prince', vivid red-orange; 'Triumph Red', clear bright red.
Mixtures: 'Carnival', creams, yellows, pinks and reds; 'Funfair', the more assertive colours only; 'Mello Red & White', reds and white in an arresting mix; 'Pastel' (syn. 'Tapestry'), the softer shades and a good blend that is easier on the eye; 'Sparklers', contains pretty well everything, including bicolours and tricolours; 'Triumph', a riot of most of the colours.

Nemophila (HA)

❝ Nemophila, *the Californian bluebell, is almost a one-variety genus for, although a handful of different types are sometimes seen, one form of* N. menziesii *puts all others in the shade. And, speaking of shade, nemophila is fairly shade tolerant and is among those annuals that really shouldn't be allowed to dry out. With its curved flowers and serrated leaves, nemophila is a delightful plant; it has been one of my annual plant discoveries of recent years.* ❞

SPECIAL FEATURES
This is a scrambling, sprawling plant that is best planted at the sides of containers so that it can tumble over the edges. It will perform more reliably than most trailing annuals in poor summers.

SUITABLE CONTAINERS
Large tubs, window boxes, hanging baskets.
HEIGHT 15–20cm (6–8in).

RECOMMENDED VARIETIES
'Baby Blue Eyes', large sky blue flowers with white centres.

Nemophila **'Baby Blue Eyes'**

Nicotiana (HHA)

❝ *Referring to nicotianas as ornamental tobacco does them something of an injustice, for they are lovely plants and don't deserve to be tarred (yes, I am aware of the inference) with the brush of this association. In saying all of this, there is one slight snag in using them as container plants in that the shorter varieties, which are more amenable to cultivation in a container, just don't have the intensity of fragrance of the tall border varieties. But then, that's life.* ❞

SPECIAL FEATURES
If the lack of fragrance of the shorter forms really is a problem, then grow the taller types, pinch them back two or three times and place them somewhere close to an open window or doorway where their scent will be appreciated on summer evenings.

SUITABLE CONTAINERS
Large tubs, small tubs.
HEIGHT 25cm (10in) for the smallest of the dwarf varieties to 1m (3ft) for border types.

RECOMMENDED VARIETIES
Large border types: 'Affinis', white flowers; 'Lime Green'; 'Sensation', mixture with star-shaped flowers which include some lovely deep reds.
Lower-growing types: 'Domino' series (F$_1$) includes 'Crimson'; 'Salmon Pink'; 'White'; 'Picotee', white and red; 'Havana' series (F$_1$) includes 'Appleblossom', white and pink bicolour; 'Lime Rose', lime green and pink bicolour.
Mixtures: 'Metro'; 'Nicki' (F$_1$); and 'Roulette' (F$_2$).

Nicotiana **'Domino Salmon Pink'**

Nierembergia (HHA/HP)

❝ *Nierembergias have been cultivated since the mid-nineteenth century, but gardeners could be forgiven for not having heard of them until relatively recently, for they were pretty rare in seed calatogues. Then an award-winning white form of the South American N. repens burst upon the scene and everyone wanted it. It has a mass of cup-shaped flowers over a mat of green foliage. One or other of the rich purple species is now pretty widely available too and they have joined my list of indispensible half-hardy annuals.* ❞

SPECIAL FEATURES

Reduce humidity and increase ventilation once the seedlings have germinated as they are prone to damping-off.

SUITABLE CONTAINERS

Large tubs, small tubs, window boxes, hanging baskets.
HEIGHT 15–20cm (6–8in).

RECOMMENDED VARIETIES

'Mont Blanc', white with gold centres, is seen in almost every catalogue. You may also find *N. hippomanica violacea* 'Purple Robe'.

Nolana (HHA/TP)

❝ *Nolanas have a good deal in common with nierembergias. They are South American, there are blue- and white-flowered varieties, they have trumpet-shaped flowers, and some gardeners have never heard of them. However, once you grow them, summer visitors to your garden will invariably ask, 'What is that, and where can I get it?'* ❞

SPECIAL FEATURES

Take cuttings in late summer and pot them up to produce attractive house plants for flowering in early spring.

SUITABLE CONTAINERS

Window boxes, small tubs, large tubs, hanging baskets.
HEIGHT 15–25cm (6–10in).

Nolana paradoxa '**Blue Bird**'

RECOMMENDED VARIETIES:

Nolana paradoxa: 'Blue Bird', sky blue flowers with white centres and a golden eye; 'Shooting Star', pale blue with darker blue, star-like centres; 'Snow Bird', white with a small yellow eye.

Osteospermum (HHA)

❝ *You can be forgiven for being confused over the group of plants commonly known as the Stars of the Veldt. These South African daisies flit easily between the genera Osteospermum and Dimorphotheca but it is worth looking under both names in your catalogues. They share the advantages and the drawbacks of other South African daisies – looking superb in warm sunshine, but sad in wet, dull weather.* ❞

SPECIAL FEATURES:

Check the varieties carefully, as some are much taller border annuals, and be sure to pinch them back.

SUITABLE CONTAINERS

Small/large tubs, window boxes.
HEIGHT 30–45cm (12–18in).

RECOMMENDED VARIETIES:

'Glistening White', pure white; 'Salmon Queen', shades of peach and apricot; 'Starshine', mixture of pink and white; 'Tetra Polestar', silver-white with purple edge.

Osteospermum '**Glistening White**'

Pelargonium (HHA/TP)

❝ I think that we have finally reached the stage where gardeners have realized that pelargoniums are the half-hardy counterparts of geraniums, a process that has undoubtedly been accelerated by the development and availability of F_1 hybrid varieties of pelargonium that can be raised from seed.

There have been two consequences, however, that have affected the development of seed-raised hybrid pelargoniums in recent years: first, many more gardeners now grow pelargoniums (which have taken on an even more important role in public bedding displays). Second, it is sad, but many of the old zonal forms with attractively patterned foliage, which must be perpetuated by cuttings, have disappeared. Nonetheless, specialist nurseries have rescued some of these and, coincidentally, have made available many more of the scented-leaf varieties which tend to have small flowers. Although strictly tender perennials, I've included a selection of these lovely plants here too.

I freely confess that I like pelargoniums and use a good many of them in my containers, but with two provisos: some of the colours, especially among the reds, are very assertive; and some of the flowers are fairly feeble so you must choose carefully. For both of these reasons, pelargoniums tend to look their best, I think, in containers rather than in garden beds (municipal parks and traffic islands are a different matter). Bear in mind that they must have heat from very early in the season to make raising them from seed worthwhile; they are among those bedding plants for which the availability of young plantlets from seed companies has been a real boon. You may be tempted by F_2 hybrid seed mixtures which cost less than the F_1 types. The economy isn't all that it seems, however, for the F_2 hybrids are of much less certain and uniform appearance and you will obtain a mixture of colours. ❞

Pelargonium **'Multibloom Salmon'**

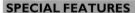

SPECIAL FEATURES

I find that the best way to make use of my greenhouse space is to overwinter a number of stock plants from the previous year's raising. These will be in flower by the time they are put outside in late spring and they can then form either the centre-piece to displays in large containers or they can simply be used as specimen plants in individual pots. This will provide an attractive display until the current season's plants come into flower a month or so later. Seed-raised plants require six months from sowing to flowering.

SUITABLE CONTAINERS
Large tubs, small tubs, window boxes, hanging baskets.
HEIGHT 20–30cm (8–12in).

RECOMMENDED VARIETIES

Ivy-leaved trailing varieties: derived from *Pelargonium peltatum*: only a few are available, including the mixture 'Summer Showers', white, pinks, red and purple; and the single colours 'Felix', white; and 'Sheba', pink-mauve.

Zonal varieties: complex hybrids, many of the modern zonals do not have the traditional patterned leaves, and there are important subdivisions, sometimes given different names by different companies:

Standard or **Specimen types:** single flowers in a few fairly large heads; including 'Century Appleblossom', soft pink; 'Horizon Deep Scarlet', probably the brightest red, if that is what you want; 'Orange Appeal', the closest to a true orange; 'Orbit White', probably the best of rather few whites.

Cascading types: half-way to trailing, with branches bearing the individual flowers arching outwards from the base. The best are the 'Breakaway' series among which 'Breakaway Red' and 'Breakaway Salmon' stand out.

Multibloom types: with ten or more compact, rounded heads of flowers in bloom simultaneously. Notable varieties are 'Multibloom White', 'Multibloom Salmon' and 'Multibloom Pink'.

Floribunda or **Patio types:** smaller, more compact and with many heads of individually fewer flowers. They include the 'Sensation' series, among which the best is 'Sensation Blush Pink'.

Among the many varieties that cannot be raised from seed but make lovely container plants are the following few, all personal favourites:

Scented leaved varieties: 'Attar of Roses', grey-green leaves, pink flowers, rose scent; 'Fragrans', soft grey-green leaves, small white flowers, pine scent; 'Lilian Pottinger', soft grey-green leaves, small white flowers, pine scent; 'Prince of Orange', dark green leaves, pale purple flowers, orange scent.

Zonal leaved varieties: 'Dolly Vardon', green and red leaves with cream edge, red flowers; 'Mr Henry Cox', dark green and red leaves with cream edge, pink flowers.

Double-flowered varieties: 'King of Denmark', salmon pink.

Rosebud varieties (very tight double flowers): 'Appleblossom Rosebud', white with green centre and pink edges.

Dwarf and Miniature varieties: 'Ambrose', cream white with pink flush; 'Emma Hossler', pink; 'Honeywood Suzanne', white with salmon pink flush.

Ivy-leaved varieties: 'L'elégante', variegated leaves and mauve flowers; 'Santa Paula', mauve.

Regal varieties (large, showy flowers, best known as house plants): 'Green Woodpecker', pale lilac with purple markings; 'Lord Bute', deep purple with pink edge.

Pelargonium **'Lord Bute'**

Pelargonium **'Summer Showers'**

Pelargonium **'Dolly Varden'**

Petunia (HHA/TP)

" Petunias are the mainstays of window boxes and containers for many gardeners every summer. Undeniably, they have a great deal to commend them: their big and cheerful flowers in a wide range of colours (although, I confess, I find some of the bicolours utterly disgusting), and excellent weather resistance (if you choose your varieties carefully). But they have two drawbacks: they are not particularly easy to raise from seed and also they must be deadheaded constantly if they are to continue blooming. However, until you are pretty experienced at raising plants from seed, you may find that you fare better buying the young plants for your containers. Indeed, with certain varieties, you will have no choice in this matter as the seed simply isn't available. "

SPECIAL FEATURES

Different gardeners work out their own ways of coping with the very tiny seed and the need to keep the compost moist. I have found the most reliable method is to use a soil-free compost, carefully firmed into the seed tray. Mix the seed thoroughly with a little vermiculite, scatter this evenly over the surface, water it with a mist sprayer, firm again and then cover. Incubate the seed tray at a temperature of 20–22°C (68–72°F) and then use the mist sprayer daily to maintain the essential dampness.

SUITABLE CONTAINERS
Hanging baskets, window boxes, large tubs.
HEIGHT 20–30cm (8–12in), depending on type.

Petunia 'Mirage Sugar'

Petunia 'Birthday Celebration' and *Verbena* 'Loveliness'

My preference is for single-coloured single flowers, but I consider here the better varieties in each group.

'Multiflora' F₁ hybrid types: the 'Carpet' series includes a charming cream 'Carpet Buttermilk', as well as individual colours and mixtures, such as: 'Carpet Mixed', white, blue, deep purple, pinks and red; 'Summertime Carpet' (including 'Buttermilk' with various blues); 'Plum Pudding Mixed', deep colours; 'Satin and Silk', pale blue, pale pink and white.

'Grandiflora' F₁ hybrid types: the 'Falcon' series includes 'Salmon', 'Pastel Salmon', 'Mid-Blue', 'White' and 'Red'; 'Birthday Celebration', pale lilac; 'Brass Band' and 'Californian Girl', both yellow; 'Blue Frost', deep blue-purple with white-edged wavy petals, awful;

'Red Picotee', vivid scarlet with white-edged wavy petals – very bright; 'Razzle Dazzle', a rather terrifying mixture of lurid bicolours.

The 'Supercascade' range has flowers in softer colours: 'Blue', 'Lilac', 'Blush'; two shades of pink, 'White' and 'Salmon'; the 'Daddy' range has some individual colours and a mixture (all veined); 'Telstar' defies belief, with blue-purple and white stripes; 'Starship Mixed' includes other striped colours.

Floribunda F₁ hybrid types: the 'Mirage' series has replaced the well known 'Resisto' range. Presently available are 'Red'; 'Rose'; 'Blue'; 'White'; 'Lilac'; 'Lavender'; 'Midnight', dark blue; 'Summer', veined salmon pink; 'Sugar', veined purple; and the mixture, 'Mirage Reflections'. The 'Celebrity' range includes 'Chiffon Morn', pale pink,

with several different mixtures, amongst which 'Celebrity Applause', a blend of white, lilacs and blue, stands out; 'Niagara', white with shades of blue and lilac.

Double F₁ hybrid types: 'Delight', single and bicolours; 'Duo Mixture', white, pinks, red, deep mauve and silver; 'Purple Pirouette', extraordinary large, purple flowers with white picotee edge; 'Strawberry Tart', the name says it all, a sickly blend of reddish-pink and white; 'Super Fanfare', a double Grandiflora mixture including bicolours.

The main group of petunias that can't be raised from seed is a fairly recent and interesting introduction, the Surfinia range. These trailing plants, suitable for hanging baskets, are available in a range of colours.

Salpiglossis (HHA)

❝ *There are plenty of good gardeners who won't trouble themselves with salpiglossis, considering them suitable only for the cool greenhouse. Salpiglossis are certainly less amenable to outdoor cultivation than their South American relatives, petunias, and I wouldn't attempt to use them as bedding plants. But in containers, they can be positioned where they won't be buffeted by the wind, despite their rather large size, and their exotic and spectacular trumpet flowers can be appreciated. They need positioning with care, but it is care worth taking.* ❞

SPECIAL FEATURES

Place the pots in a warm, but not too hot, sheltered situation. Push canes into the pots and give a little wrap-around support with soft garden twine.

To my knowledge, single colours aren't available. You have the choice of several F₁ hybrid mixtures: 'Festival', 'Flamenco' and 'Carnival' – with different blends of golden yellow, red, purple, mauve and pink with darker veining. Cheaper F₂ mixtures are also available, but the plants are really much too tall for containers.

Salpiglossis **'Festival'**

SUITABLE CONTAINERS

Large tubs, small tubs.
HEIGHT 30–45cm (12–18in).

Salvia (HHA/TP)

  ❝ You either like them or you quite definitely don't. The tall, soldier-like, mainly bright red forms of the Brazilian Salvia splendens *seem to have passed their peak of popularity as bedding plants. Perhaps this is because modern pelargoniums will supply a bigger, more uniform and generally brighter display. However, salvias have their devotees and I believe they do have a role to play in containers provided you choose the shorter-growing varieties. I still think they look terrible in window boxes; looking out of a room with a window box of salvias outside must be like looking out through prison bars. ❞*

SPECIAL FEATURES

Try to blend salvias with plants of rather cooler colours such as soft pinks and powder blues, ageratum, for example. This won't diminish their impact but sets them off more attractively. They just look stark on their own.

Salvia 'Red Rivers'

SUITABLE CONTAINERS

Large tubs.
HEIGHT 25–35cm (10–14in).

RECOMMENDED VARIETIES

'Blaze of Fire', 'Firecracker', 'Phoenix Red' and 'Scarlet King' are the best I have grown in containers because of their relatively neat, compact habit. 'Red River' and 'Scarlet Signal' are good but slightly taller. If you want other colours, try the fairly low-growing 'Phoenix Purple'. There are also mixtures such as 'Phoenix Mixed' that include some peculiar pinks, and 'Pharoah Mixed' about which little should be said save that it includes bicolours.

Schizanthus (HHA)

  ❝ Poor man's orchid and butterfly flower are familiar names for schizanthus, a plant that, like nicotianas, petunias and many other pretty things, belongs unexpectedly to the potato family. Their names do make it sound like a plant trying to be something that it isn't. Some people think it is only trying to be an outdoor summer annual and that its real function is as a splendid pot plant for the cool greenhouse. My view is that, yes, schizanthus is a fine greenhouse plant but that the lower-growing forms also make attractive additions to outdoor containers. ❞

SPECIAL FEATURES

Although schizanthus exist only as mixtures in a riot of colours, they are soft and gentle colours and, because the flowers are individually small, they never look vulgar.

SUITABLE CONTAINERS

Large tubs, small tubs, window boxes.
HEIGHT 20–35cm (8–14in).

RECOMMENDED VARIETIES

Low-growing mixtures: 'Star Parade', probably the neatest, most compact form; 'Dwarf Bouquet' and 'Disco' (an F_2 hybrid). 'Angel Wings' and 'Hit Parade' are taller.

Schizanthus 'Dwarf Bouquet'

Tagetes Marigold (HHA)

I have been through phases with marigolds – I used to grow big ones, then I went right off them, considering them far too brash and vulgar. Now I find some of the smaller types, especially the single-flowered forms, both pretty and useful in containers. Unlike the pot marigolds or calendulas (see page 22), all are half-hardy. They are generally divided into those derived from Tagetes erecta*, known as African marigolds, and those* derived from T. patula*, known as French marigolds. The African varieties are generally of little use for containers. The French types are lower-growing, less bushy with single, semi-double or double flowers. The plants traditionally called tagetes are forms of* T. tenuifolia*, and are low growing with feathery foliage and masses of orange-yellow single flowers. It is to these and the single French varieties that I have now returned.*

SPECIAL FEATURES
All are among the easiest of half-hardy annuals to raise from seed. The seed is large, germinates easily and produces quick-growing and tough seedlings, seldom prone to damping-off.

RECOMMENDED VARIETIES
Rather than give meaningless lists here, I shall indicate the features of the main subdivisions of dwarf French marigolds and tagetes that you will generally see in catalogues. Dwarf French Double or Carnation Flowered are fully double, compact, free-flowering; Dwarf French Crested are single or double with the central petals rolled upwards in a crest; Dwarf French Single are not always very dwarfed, reaching up to 30cm (12in), fairly compact, free-flowering and excellent for containers; Afro-French F_1 hybrids, up to 40cm (16in), single or double; Tagetes, up to 25cm (10in), single, excellent for containers.

SUITABLE CONTAINERS
Large/small tubs, window boxes.
HEIGHT 15–40cm (6–16in).

Tagetes 'Golden Gem'

Thunbergia (HHA/TP)

Good annual climbers are to be cherished; and thunbergia is to be cherished more than most. It's a charming plant from tropical Africa that I discovered a good many years ago when I was entranced by its single, smiling orange flowers and its restrained climbing habit. Sadly, in the cause of 'improvement', many seed companies now offer only mixtures and the pure clear colour of the true species is hard to find.

SPECIAL FEATURES
Thunbergia won't trail, so grow it by all means in hanging baskets but you should expect it to grow upwards, clinging to the support chains, not downwards. I think it is at its best when grown in tubs with wigwam support.

SUITABLE CONTAINERS
Small tubs, hanging baskets.
HEIGHT 1m (3ft).

RECOMMENDED VARIETIES
I am in no doubt that the true species *Thunbergia alata* with orange flowers and a black eye is better than the mixture called 'Susie' which is now more generally offered. 'Susie' includes yellow and white, and even some flowers without a black eye, which is not particularly good for a plant whose common name is black-eyed Susan. Choose a good colour from the mixture and perpetuate it by taking cuttings.

Tropaeolum Nasturtium (HHA/TP)

" I've said before that the South American Tropaeolum *is probably the single most useful genus of annual and herbaceous climbers and two groups provide valuable container plants: the red or orange-flowered nasturtiums (derived mainly from* T. majus*) which exist as dwarf, so-called semi-trailing and climbing forms; and the yellow canary creeper,* T. peregrinum. *The first is a genuine annual and the second, a tender perennial. They are especially attractive in hanging baskets. "*

SPECIAL FEATURES

The two nasturtium species are best when set against lush foliage to show off their colours. Both will trail from hanging baskets although semi-trailing nasturtiums are better at this than canary creeper which likes to climb.

SUITABLE CONTAINERS

Dwarf and semi-trailing forms: large/small tubs, window boxes.
Semi-trailing and possibly climbing forms: hanging baskets.
HEIGHT Dwarf and semi-trailing forms 20–35cm (8–14in). Climbing forms 2–3m (6½–10ft).

Tropaeolum peregrinum

RECOMMENDED VARIETIES

Dwarf nasturtiums: most seed companies have their own mixtures such as 'Jewel', yellow, orange and red-flowered plants. The 'Whirlybird' series is excellent, available as a mixture and also as individual cream, scarlet, gold and orange. The 'Alaska' series, a dwarf range of similar colours combined with speckled foliage. The most common semi-trailing types are the 'Gleam' series, generally mixtures.

Verbena (HHA/TP)

" Not so long ago, verbenas were always raised from cuttings but a considerable number of varieties can now be grown from seed as half-hardy annuals. Most gardeners still prefer to buy plants and let the nurseries cope with their awkward germination needs. Verbenas with their rather neat trailing habit, pretty feathery foliage and compact flowers are high on my list of invaluable container annuals, although they should be used sparingly to complement other things; two or three only per hanging basket. "

SPECIAL FEATURES

The trick to good germination is not to water the compost after the seeds have been sown. Dampen it first, sow the seeds on the surface, place a propagator cover over the top, maintain a temperature of around 21–22°C (70–72°F) and place it somewhere dark, or cover the whole thing with brown paper.

SUITABLE CONTAINERS

Hanging baskets, window boxes, large tubs, small tubs.
HEIGHT Those I recommend are not very tall: 15–30cm (6–12in).

RECOMMENDED VARIETIES

There are two groups of verbena hybrids for raising from seed: the spreading type and the more compact, upright type. The best compact forms are 'Blaze' and 'Sandy Scarlet', bright red; 'Blue Lagoon', clear blue; while 'Derby' and 'Celebration' are fine mixtures. The best spreading types are 'Silver Wedding', pale lilac; 'Imagination', rich purple; and 'Peaches and Cream'. If you buy verbenas as plants, try 'Sissinghurst', deep-pink; 'Silver Anne', pale- and mid-pink; and 'White Knight'.

Viola (HA/HP)

> *There can't be any more fondly loved garden plants than pansies and violas with their cheerful smiling faces and they are quite invaluable as container plants, especially during the winter months. The botanical differences between pansies, violas and violets are a bit complex and relate to the wild species from which they originated. As far as container gardening is concerned, it's easiest to divide them into those that flower through the winter and into early spring, and those that flower in late spring and summer. There is some overlap between the varieties chosen for these roles; for flowers in winter and early spring, the seeds are sown and the plants planted in summer and autumn (they are therefore in the garden through the winter), while for essentially summer-flowering plants, you should sow the seed in spring.*

Viola 'Universal'

SPECIAL FEATURES

The winter-flowering pansy has truly leapt to the fore as a winter colour plant, but it is important to place it somewhere sunny. Don't be dispirited when their heads bow low in frosty weather; they will rise again. It's also important to ensure that the plants are in flower by the time they are planted in the autumn; so sow early if you are raising your own, or pay more for larger plants if you are buying them.

SUITABLE CONTAINERS

Window boxes, large tubs, small tubs, hanging baskets.
HEIGHT 15–20cm (6–8in).

RECOMMENDED VARIETIES

Winter flowering: choose individual colours of 'Winter flowering' or 'Universal F_1' pansies (I have seen about 12 distinct types) under whatever colour names the seed companies offer them; if you really can't find these individual colours, then choose 'Universal Mixture' or 'Ultima Mixed' (which claims 25 different colours) in preference to the 'Floral Dance' range.

Spring/summer flowering: 'Universal' types will suffice for early spring; for late spring and early summer, try the following single colours: 'Moonlight', primrose yellow; 'Padparadja', beautiful rich orange; 'Royal Delft', cream and violet; 'Ullswater', deep blue with very dark blue blotch; or the 'Imperial' range including 'Light Blue', 'Purple' and 'Pink'. If you want something that no-one could ignore, try 'Jolly Joker', deep purple with a bright orange centre; 'Rippling Waters', dark purple verging on black with a white picotee edge.

Smaller-flowered 'viola' types for smaller summer containers: 'Baby Lucia', bright sky blue, an exquisite plant; 'Prince Henry', purple with gold markings; 'Prince John', golden yellow – I think this is the same as another variety called 'Yellow Prince'.

Verbena 'Sissinghurst'

TENDER PERENNIALS

Many of the subjects in this section are better known as houseplants, and it's perfectly possible for the two roles to be combined so that the plant goes outdoors in a container in the summer. All these plants must be taken under protection at the end of the outdoor season and, while many will merely be kept as stock plants in the greenhouse to be used again in the following spring, or as the source of cuttings, some can certainly be taken indoors.

Begonia sutherlandii

Argyranthemum

66 *Most people still wouldn't be able to name an argyranthemum if they tripped over it; the chances are they would still call it a marguerite. It is a species that seems to belong in a container; rarely are these plants seen in the open garden. In mild areas, the standard plants, with their masses of white, golden-centred daisy flowers, will stay outdoors all year round; in colder areas they should be overwintered in a cool greenhouse.* 99

SPECIAL FEATURES

The prettiest way to grow marguerites is as standards, pinching out the side-shoots in much the same way as for fuchsias (see page 45). New plants are obtained most readily by semi-hardwood cuttings taken in summer.

SUITABLE CONTAINERS
Small tubs.
HEIGHT About 1m (3ft).

RECOMMENDED VARIETIES
TIn addition to the white *Argyranthemum frutescens*, there's the double 'Album Plenum' and a lovely related variety 'Jamaica Primrose'.

Begonia

66 *I think of* Begonia *as one of the most valuable tender genera of plants for container-growing, although it includes species that must be raised in different ways. True tender perennials include those that I call 'proper' tuberous begonias: derived from several South American species, with varieties which have some of the largest, most gaudy and most assertively coloured flowers you are ever likely to see. Second, there is a range of varieties, most commonly seen as house plants, some of which have a useful trailing habit and others have very striking leaf patterns and colours.* 99

SPECIAL FEATURES

They must be deadheaded regularly, because individual flowers are not long-lived, and both look untidy and attract mould when they fade. The stems are almost invariably brittle; thus begonias shouldn't be placed in an exposed site.

SUITABLE CONTAINERS
Hanging baskets, window boxes, large tubs.
HEIGHT Varies considerably with type (see below).

RECOMMENDED VARIETIES

Tuberous types: Large-flowered forms are generally called *Begonia* x *tuberhybrida*; these varieties usually reach 30cm (12in). They include single- and double-flowered, frilled and crested forms, plus types of plant with camellia-, carnation-, rosebud- and narcissus-like flowers and smaller-flowered pendulous forms, trailing up to 1m (3ft). Colours include pinks and reds, yellows, oranges and whites. Among other tuberous begonias, *B. sutherlandii* is lovely in hanging baskets.

Non-tuberous types: The *Begonia rex* group, reaching up to 60cm (24in), includes many varieties with large, heart-shaped, sometimes markedly hairy leaves in stunning patterns of greens, reds and purples; usually these plants have small white or pink flowers. *B. masoniana* is similar but has a cross pattern on the puckered leaves. *B.* 'Tiger' is a small bushy plant, reaching up to 35cm (14in) in height and has deep purple- and green-spotted leaves and little white flowers.

Fuchsia

A very dear friend, a fine and distinguished naturalist could never see eye-to-eye with me on the subject of fuchsias. He felt that no garden flower so distorted nature's intentions. In trying to win him over by showing him my collection of species fuchsias, I played into his hands. With their small, rather neat and often sparse flowers, commonly dark red, they were so different from the large-flowered, gaudily coloured hanging basket hybrids. And I confess that I have some problems with fuchsias, too. As will be evident, I love the species but I have to concede that they are of somewhat esoteric interest, and in containers are likely to be swamped by the other plants. I also find it hard to come to terms with some of the vivid red and white bicolours. They are, however, extremely useful as container plants and are also almost classic tender perennials.

SUITABLE CONTAINERS

Hanging baskets, large tubs, small tubs, window boxes.

HEIGHT Varies widely, but this is hardly surprising as the wild species range from creeping plants of almost alpine habit to small trees. Most of the bushy forms for garden containers reach 30cm (12in) to 60cm (24in) within a season; the cascading basket types will trail to similar distances.

SPECIAL FEATURES

I always retain a few plants of each bush or upright variety every year and over-winter them in the cool greenhouse. Then cut them back by two-thirds in early spring to produce new shoots for taking cuttings, and use them individually as feature plants. Be sure to use the right varieties for each situation, and especially to use only the pendulous basket types in hanging baskets.

Fuchsia 'Tennessee Waltz'

A standard fuchsia can be stunning

Fuchsia 'Annabel'

RECOMMENDED VARIETIES

Where more than one colour is indicated in the following descriptions, the first denotes the tube and sepals, the second the corolla. See the illustrations on page 45 for examples of semi-double and double flower types.

Basket or cascade varieties:
'Cascade', single, white with pink flush/rich pink; 'Eva Boerg', not strictly a basket variety but very good in hanging baskets, double, white-pinkish/purple with pink splashes; 'Golden Marinka', single, bright red/slightly darker red, variegated green and yellow foliage; 'Harry Gray', double, pale pink-white/white-pale pink; 'Jack Shahan', single, deep pink; 'La Campanella', semi-double, pinkish white/purple;

'Marinka', single, bright red/slightly darker red; 'Orange Crystal', single, orange; 'Pink Galore', double, pink/pink with green tips; 'Quasar', double, white/violet with white base; 'Spion Kop', double, reddish pink/white with pink veins; 'Swingtime', double, scarlet/white with red veins, probably the most popular of all fuchsias.

Bush or upright varieties: 'Abbé Farges', semi-double, pale cherry red/lilac; 'Alice Hoffman', single, rose pink/white with pink veins; 'Annabel' double, very pale pink/white; 'Beacon', single, scarlet/mauve-pink; 'Billy Green', triphylla, salmon pink; 'Brutus', single, deep red-scarlet/purple; 'Celia Smedley', single, rich pink-white/red; 'Checkerboard',

single, rich red-white/red with white base; 'Display', single, pink/deep pink; 'Dollar Princess', double, dark red/purple; 'Heidi Ann', double, red/lilac-purple; 'Lady Thumb', semi-double, red/white with pink veining; 'Madame Cornelissen', semi-double, crimson/white with crimson veins; 'Margaret Brown', single, deep pink/pale pink; 'Nellie Nuttall', erect single, red/white; 'Phyllis', semi-double, shades of reddish-pink; 'Snowcap', semi-double, scarlet/white with red veins; 'Tennessee Waltz', semi-double, rich pink/lilac with pink spotting; 'Thalia', triphylla, red/orange scarlet, rich, velvety dark purple-olive leaves – my favourite fuchsia and a superb specimen for a large pot.

STANDARD FUCHSIAS

Standard forms of plants always attract attention and fascination, and standard fuchsias are no exception. A well grown specimen in an attractive pot makes a fine centre-piece for a display of container plants, or can be a feature on its own in a gravelled or paved courtyard. You can buy 'ready-made' standards from garden centres but you will pay fairly handsomely for the privilege. It is much more rewarding to train your own. Some varieties are more suitable than others. It is important to choose one with strong, upright growth; among the best I have used are 'Checkerboard', 'Snowcap' and 'Tennessee Waltz' but feel free to experiment for yourself. 'Abbé

Farges' is particularly good for shorter standards (see below).

It is possible to make weeping standards with a basket variety but this is a longer and trickier task, and so I suggest you gain practice first with upright types.

Look carefully at your available plants (or at those in the local garden centre) and, if you find one with three instead of the usual two leaves at each node, choose it: it will naturally make a more compact head. Take a strong cutting in the usual way and insert a cane support. Once the cutting has rooted and is producing side-shoots, pinch these out, allowing the stem leaves to remain in place. Don't pinch out the stem tip until the plant has

reached the desired height– which can be whatever you choose, although, technically, the height from compost to the base of the head is 75cm–1.1m (30in–3½ft) for a full Standard, 45–75cm (18–30in) for a Half-standard, 25–45cm (10–18in) for a Quarter-standard and 15–25cm (6–10in) for a Mini-standard. Ideally, the finished plant should have a head twice the height of the bare stem. Form the head by repeatedly pinching out the shoots within it at every third pair of leaves. You can keep your standard from year to year in a cool greenhouse. Cut back the crown just as you would with a normal bush plant, but leave the stem intact.

Gerbera

" A colleague of mine thinks that gerberas look like dandelions when they have finished flowering, but as long as they don't look like them before, I don't mind. They are unmistakably members of the daisy family. The flowers are usually bright orange rather than bright yellow. These plants can be raised from seed and treated as annuals, in which case a wider colour range is available, but I always find this less satisfactory than buying selected strains and growing them as true perennials. "

SPECIAL FEATURES

Gerberas are evergreen, herbaceous plants which must not be allowed to die down in winter. I keep mine in individual pots under the greenhouse bench, watering and feeding them monthly; later I put them in large containers, although still in their own pots. Despite their South African origins, they don't like very hot, sunny positions.

Gerbera jamesonii

SUITABLE CONTAINERS
Window boxes, large tubs.
HEIGHT 45–60cm (18–24in).

RECOMMENDED VARIETIES

The normal orange-flowered species is G. *jamesonii* and, although the cultivated plants sold under this name will probably be hybrids, this is the form you will see most commonly at garden centres. You may also see plants in other colours that have been raised from one of the seed mixtures or dwarf strains such as 'Happipot'.

Helichrysum petiolare

Helichrysum

" The daisy genus Helichrysum *is a big and important one, embracing over 500 species, mostly from South Africa. These plants mean different things to different gardeners, and you may well be familiar with the species raised annually from seed as one form of 'everlasting flowers' for drying. These could, I suppose, be used in containers but far more important in our context are a couple of perennial species (see right), grown not for their flowers but for their trailing stems, with more or less rounded silver-woolly leaves, which make a perfect foil for flowering container plants. "*

SPECIAL FEATURES

These woolly helichrysums aren't easy to overwinter in a cool greenhouse, for they are likely to die back and rot in cold conditions. It is essential to keep them and their compost on the dry side. Assuming you are able to overwinter stock plants, you may find it more effective to layer the shoots for propagation in the spring rather than to take cuttings: rotting, once again, is a major problem in a humid propagator.

SUITABLE CONTAINERS
Window boxes, hanging baskets, large tubs.
HEIGHT 1.5m (5ft), trailing.

RECOMMENDED VARIETIES

There are two main species: the larger-leaved, 4cm (1½in)-diameter H. *petiolare* (which is sometimes called H. *petiolatum*), and the smaller-leaved, 1cm (½in)-diameter, neater H. *microphyllum* (which is now more correctly called *Plecostachys serpyllifolia*). Common variants of the former are 'Limelight', with lime-green leaves, and 'Variegatum', which has a grey-cream variegation.

Lantana

❝ I've lost count of the number of times people have asked me the name of an attractive shrub they've seen growing along a Mediterranean seafront. The shrub is lantana and, like many another tender shrub, it makes an excellent container plant. There are numerous colour selections, and their striking effect arises because, within each flower head, the individual blooms mature at different times and their colours change as they do so. ❞

SPECIAL FEATURES

It is possible to raise lantanas from seed, but it is better to buy named varieties and treat them like fuchsias (see page 45), taking cuttings each spring. They make attractive standards. Lantanas are tolerant of very hot conditions, but if kept in these conditions an infestation by red spider mites may result.

SUITABLE CONTAINERS

Hanging baskets, large tubs.

HEIGHT As shrubs in mild areas, these will reach about 1.5–2m (5–6½ft) but grown each year from cuttings, they will trail to about 45–60cm (18–24in).

RECOMMENDED VARIETIES

Plants sold for hanging baskets and other containers are two South American species: *L. camara* has red, yellow or orange flowers and *L. montevidensis* mauve or purple, although among its attractive ariants are: 'Brasier', vivid red; 'Mr Bessieres', pink and yellow; 'Snow White', white. Given a warm greenhouse or conservatory it would be worth growing on one or two plants as specimens.

Lantana camara

Nepeta *Glechoma*

❝ The plant called simply 'nepeta' has long been the favourite trailing foliage for use in hanging baskets, although the botanical genus Nepeta includes a number of attractive and useful border perennials. The hanging-basket nepeta is a related plant, but is, in fact, a variegated form of the native ground ivy, Glechoma hederacea. It is just about hardy, although unreliably so, and is thus much better treated as a tender perennial. I'm always amazed at the way that nurseries understate its vigour; I've seen many a label that gives its ultimate length as 60cm (24in) but mine regularly reaches ground level from a hanging basket at a height of nearly 2m (6½ft). ❞

SPECIAL FEATURES

After potting up a few stock plants in the autumn, cut them back to within about 30cm (12in) of the base; in the spring take cuttings in the usual way. Some people are allergic to the wild species which can cause skin rashes but I've never heard of anyone being affected by the variegated form.

SUITABLE CONTAINERS

Hanging baskets, large tubs.

HEIGHT Trailing to 1–2m (3–6½ft), depending on how well it is fed.

RECOMMENDED VARIETIES

The form to use is 'Variegata'; you are unlikely to see any other.

Passiflora

66 *Few blooms excite as much admiration as those of passion flowers, and it always comes as a surprise to realize that a plant quite so exotic in appearance can also be hardy. But the hardy passion flower,* Passiflora caerulea, *is only one species in an incredibly beautiful genus; and, given some means of overwinter protection, numerous others can make stunning container subjects.* 99

SPECIAL FEATURES

Ideally passion flowers are best when supported by a stout framework in a large pot, and should be cut back by a quarter of their old growth each spring before being put outside. If the plants become too big to manage, cut them back to 1m (3ft) above the compost. Some species are herbaceous, and die down naturally to a rootstock each year. All will flower best if extraneous shoots are pinched out regularly during the summer, and if they are fed with a fertilizer with a high potash content.

SUITABLE CONTAINERS
Large tubs.
HEIGHT Most of those I recommend below will reach about 2m (6½ft) each season if cut back moderately hard.

RECOMMENDED VARIETIES

P. antioquiensis, vivid red; *P. x caeruleoracemosa*, red with white and purple bands; *P. edulis*, green and white; *P. exoniensis*, red, pink and violet; *P. mollissima*, pink; *P. quadrangularis*, green, pink and mauve; a large and vigorous plant.

Passiflora antioquiensis

Plectranthus

66 *Popularly called the Swedish ivy, presumably because the Swedes must like it and its leaves are roughly like those of a small-leaved ivy; this is one of the easiest and most popular of trailing foliage house plants. Yet it and its relatives make very good subjects for hanging baskets or other containers for one sound reason: they are tolerant of shade. They have only one drawback: their stems are rather brittle, so it is best to position them somewhere that people will not brush against them.* 99

SPECIAL FEATURES

Avoid hot, dry and sunny conditions, as the plants will respond both by not growing and by turning a sickly purple.

Plectranthus oertendahlii

SUITABLE CONTAINERS
Hanging baskets, window boxes.
HEIGHT
Varies with species, but most will trail to 60cm–1m (24in–3ft) within a year from cuttings.

RECOMMENDED VARIETIES

My favourite species is *P. australis*, which has plain but lush green, glossy leaves; however, you are more likely to see: *P. forsteri* 'Marginatus', large leaves with cream variegation; *P. madagascariensis* (variegated mintleaf), fragrant, variegated leaves; *P. oertendahlii*, purple beneath, green with white veins above.

Rhodochiton

❝ *I once told a colleague who professed a liking for* Rhodochiton *that he must also like whitefly, because no other plant I have ever grown in a greenhouse has attracted more of them. But, to be fair, that was in a greenhouse. Used as an outdoor container plant (as it is much less frequently), this little purple-flowered Mexican climber offers rather a different prospect. The flowers are curiously appealing; they look rather like parachutes, although you need to be able to look up at them to appreciate the parachutist beneath.* ❞

SPECIAL FEATURES
Rhodochiton can be raised from seed, but I have never found this particularly easy. By far the best bet is to buy a plant, take cuttings to multiply the stock, and then overwinter it in a cool greenhouse, like any other tender perennial (the whitefly are significantly less active at that time of year).

SUITABLE CONTAINERS
Hanging baskets, large tubs.
HEIGHT Depending on the mildness of the area and the warmth of the season, in a container rhodochitons can sometimes reach about 2m (6½ft) within a season.

RECOMMENDED VARIETIES
Only the normal species, *R. atrosanguineum*, is usually available.

Scaevola

❝ *Not very many Australian plants find their way into our summer containers, and certainly not many Australian perennials. Sadly, even this one doesn't find its way into as many containers as I think it should. It is still sold most frequently as a house plant or conservatory species, but* S. aemula *occurs naturally on sand dunes. This must explain why it is so good in hanging baskets where the free drainage is comparable and its drought tolerance a great advantage. Do grow it: I can guarantee your friends will say 'What is it?' and 'May I have a cutting?'; generally in that order.* ❞

SPECIAL FEATURES
Because they are also very successful houseplants, scaevolas are among those useful plants that can be overwintered as attractive specimens in the home after their summer in the garden. They therefore make a good choice for container gardening even if you don't have a greenhouse.

SUITABLE CONTAINERS
Hanging baskets, window boxes.
HEIGHT Will trail to 60cm (24in).

RECOMMENDED VARIETIES
The variety you will generally see is 'Blue Fan' although there are other blue-flowered forms as well as, predictably, a white variant, 'Alba'.

Rhodochiton atrosanguineum

Scaevola aemula 'Blue Fan'

Tradescantia

❝ *Tradescantia is yet one more plant best known in contexts other than outdoor summer containers. The hardy* T. x andersoniana *is a familiar herbaceous border perennial, while* T. fluminensis *and its relatives are popular trailing foliage house plants. But there are lots of good reasons why you should use them to trail in hanging baskets, too, and, just like scaevolas, they can be taken indoors at the end of the summer.*

Gardeners often imagine that tradescantias belong to the lily family but in truth they are in a large and important warm climate group called the Commelinaceae which very surprisingly has almost no other cultivated ornamentals of note. ❞

SPECIAL FEATURES
Be careful when using tradescantias in hanging baskets for two reasons: first, they are among the more brittle plants and it is easy to knock off lengths of stem; second, they are intolerant of waterlogging and so are best placed very close to the sides and edges of the basket when they will remain fairly dry.

SUITABLE CONTAINERS
Hanging baskets, window boxes.
HEIGHT Will trail to about 75cm (30in) within a season.

RECOMMENDED VARIETIES
The form that you will see most frequently is *T. fluminensis* which has white striped leaves, but other good and fairly widely available varieties are: 'Aurea', yellow leaves with green stripes; 'Laekenensis', white and pink striped leaves. Other colour combinations occur; perhaps the most colourful of all are the forms of *T. zebrina*, which often have purple and silver leaf colours. All still tend to be found in the houseplant department of garden centres.

Tradescantia zebrina

51

HARDY PERENNIALS

This section perhaps more than any other in this book has presented me with considerable problems concerning what I should leave out. No doubt a very large proportion of lower-growing and stiffer-stemmed herbaceous perennials could be raised perfectly well in containers, but I do not think very many have been. I know those that I describe here work well so I hope that more gardeners will experiment with this type of plant, both in mixtures and as single varieties; either method can certainly give a really stunning effect.

Ajuga

Ajugas, bugles, are common enough native plants but they are also versatile in the garden. I find them particularly useful for providing ground cover in lightly shaded places. They are almost equally valuable in containers as a foliage background to other plants, especially in the less sunny spots; I have found them particularly effective in hanging baskets. Although all varieties will generally push up spikes of blue flowers in early summer, this may not be desirable in a container planting as it can spoil the effect of other plants in the collection so don't be afraid of pinching them out.

SPECIAL FEATURES
Ajugas can be prone to mildew, and this is always worse in hot and dry situations; a further reason why you should put them in containers that are in slightly cooler, shadier places.

SUITABLE CONTAINERS
Hanging baskets, small pots, large pots.
HEIGHT Will trail to about 60cm (24in) within a season.

RECOMMENDED VARIETIES
Most of the many varieties of *A. reptans* have been selected for their leaf colour, which is generally in varying shades of bronze, green and purple. Although my favourite for garden use is 'Atropurpurea' (deep bronze-purple), perhaps the best container plant is 'Braunherz' (uniformly shiny, dark purple). 'Variegata' has a neat habit and its greyish-green leaves have cream edges; I have seen it used to good effect on its own in a large pot. The 'Jungle' varieties and 'Catlin's Giant' are widely available, but are too big and robust for containers.

Ajuga reptans **'Braunherz'**

Artemisia

Artemisias are part of the herbalist's stock-in-trade, many species having for centuries been put to medicinal use. As flowering plants, however, they have little to commend them. In spite of this apparent lack of promise, a small range of species do have considerable value for their attractive, silvery and filigree foliage and these make fine feature plants in sunny places.

SPECIAL FEATURES
The foliage will turn brown at the stem base if the compost is waterlogged.

SUITABLE CONTAINERS
Small pots, large pots.
HEIGHT Those below will reach about 75cm–1m (30in–3ft).

RECOMMENDED VARIETIES
A. absinthium 'Lambrook Silver'; *A. arborescens* 'Faith Raven'; *A.* 'Powis Castle'; *A. stelleriana* 'Mori' (also called 'Boughton Silver').

A. absinthium **'Lambrook Silver'**

Bergenia

> *I see bergenias frequently in gardens because, although never spectacular, they offer valuable ground cover for shady places. But I rarely see them in containers, other than in my own garden. This is something of a puzzle since they can provide much the same effect when grown in this way. Their large, glossy leaves make a striking display in attractive terracotta pots in a small formal courtyard.*

SPECIAL FEATURES

Although usually thought of as foliage plants, bergenias do produce flowering spikes in spring and you should make your choice in terms of leaf and flower combination. As evergreens, bergenias are especially good for all-year-round effect. Do be sure to place them out of direct hot sun and to grow them in a rich, moisture-retentive compost.

SUITABLE CONTAINERS
Small pots, large pots.
HEIGHT Will attain 45cm (18in).

RECOMMENDED VARIETIES
Hybrids: 'Abendglut', red-bronze leaves, deep red flowers; 'Baby Doll', green leaves, double, pale pink flowers; 'Bressingham Ruby', dark green leaves, turning rich red-purple in winter, dark red flowers; 'Morgenröte', small green leaves, large flowers, deep red-pink, repeat-flowering. *B. cordifolia* 'Purpurea', purple leaves, deep pink flowers.

Chrysanthemum

> *Having spent a number of years explaining to gardeners that what they knew and loved as a Chrysanthemum has become a Dendranthema, I now find myself having to retract. For the genus Chrysanthemum has been reassembled and the border and florists' chrysanthemums, banished to Dendranthema, have now returned to the fold. Whilst I still find the annual chrysanthemums to be the best container types, there is a group of perennials that I shall concentrate on here and that I find work rather well. These are the small-flowered spray chrysanthemums, so valuable for cutting when they are grown in borders.*

Chrysanthemum 'Wessex Wine'

SPECIAL FEATURES

Although notionally hardy, they suffer in cold, wet winters and are always best lifted for storage in the cold greenhouse or cold-frame. It's much simpler and more logical to grow them permanently in pots. However, they will become tall and leggy unless you pinch them back, and remove the terminal bud early in the season. Then any more terminal buds on the side-shoots should be pinched out to encourage a bushy form and more flowers.

SUITABLE CONTAINERS
Small pots, large pots.
HEIGHT If pinched back, will attain about 1m (3ft).

RECOMMENDED VARIETIES
The excellent 'Pennine' and 'Wessex' series include the full chrysanthemum range of yellows, oranges, reds, pinks, purples and whites.

Chrysanthemum 'Pennine Jewel'

Ferns

" *The principle of growing ferns in containers is exactly the same as when you grow ferns in a garden bed; provide them with a damp and fairly shady spot otherwise most species will simply fail. If you find the idea of having containers situated in a moist, shady corner of the garden appealing, no plant will fill the role as well as ferns can. I have seen hanging baskets of ferns used cunningly to provide genuine interest and appeal in the most improbable of places; places where a conventional hanging-basket planting would have rotted away in as little as a week.* "

SPECIAL FEATURES

Remember that while many ferns are deciduous, there are also evergreen (or 'wintergreen') species that can provide year-round interest.

SUITABLE CONTAINERS

Hanging baskets, small pots and large pots.

HEIGHT Ferns vary in size and you can grow whatever you choose according to the size of your container. For small pots and certainly for hanging baskets, restrict your selection to those ferns that will attain about 45cm (18in).

RECOMMENDED VARIETIES

Among the ferns I have found most suitable and easy for containers are: the forms of *Asplenium scolopendrium*, the hart's-tongue-fern, especially the wavy- and crested-leaved forms; the various evergreen species of ladder-fern (*Blechnum*); *Polypodium vulgare* 'Cornubiense', a variety of the limestone polypody, which differs from most ferns in requiring chalky conditions and in being tolerant of both sunlight and dryness; the tightly curled form of the shield fern *Polystichum setiferum* 'Divisilobum Densum'; and small neat varieties of maidenhair fern.

Geranium

" *To most gardeners geraniums equate with pelargoniums so far as containers are concerned (see page 36) and the true, hardy geraniums scarcely get a look in. This needn't and shouldn't be the case. The many virtues of at least some of these beautiful flowers can be used to as much good effect in a container as in the open garden. In choosing them, however, do bear in mind that the flowering period of the individual species isn't long, and most taller-growing border species are unsatisfactory since they require substantial support. That still leaves a considerable range of very attractive plants, including a number of useful ground cover plants.* "

SPECIAL FEATURES

Most hardy geraniums are fairly vigorous plants, and will need dividing every two or three years. I find they are also among those container plants that are best grown on their own, with the pots moved in and out of conspicuous positions as the plants come into flower. They are also among the perennials for which deadheading really is scarcely practical. The flowers are small and so the task is very fiddly; they also drop fairly quickly of their own accord.

SUITABLE CONTAINERS

Small pots, large pots.

HEIGHT The types I recommend here range from about 15cm (6in) to about 75cm (30in).

RECOMMENDED VARIETIES

G. cinereum 'Ballerina', white with red-purple markings, 15cm (6in); *G. c. subcaulescens*, magenta with black centres, 15cm (6in); *G. x lindavicum* 'Apple Blossom', pink, 15cm (6in); *G. dalmaticum*, pink, 25cm (10in); *G. x oxonianum* 'Wargrave Pink', pink, 45cm (18in); *G. himalayense*, purple, 25cm (10in); *G. phaeum*, deep purple, superb in shade and although 75cm (30in) tall, it won't require staking. *G. procurrens*, magenta, 10cm (4in); *G. pylzowianum*, pink, beautifully mottled foliage, 20cm (8in); *G. x riversleaianum* 'Russell Prichard', magenta, 20cm (8in); *G. sanguineum*, magenta, 20cm (8in); *G. s. lancastriense* 'Splendens', pink, 10–15cm (4–6in).

Aspleniums and other ferns in a small trough container

Grasses

❝ *I've already described a number of annual grasses that make excellent additions to the range of container plants, and the number of perennial grasses is comparable. Those I suggest have proved their worth to me and undoubtedly others would be as effective. But do be sure to select clump- rather than mat-forming species, and be aware that some will self-seed freely so that you need to pull out unwanted seedlings regularly from around containers.* ❞

SPECIAL FEATURES

As with annual grasses, I think you will fare best if you opt for a single species or variety rather than attempt to mix together different types of grasses, or grasses with other types of plant.

Geranium dalmaticum

Alopecurus pratensis

SUITABLE CONTAINERS
Small tubs, large tubs.
HEIGHT Varies with species.

RECOMMENDED VARIETIES

Alopecurus pratensis 'Aureomarginatus', yellow and green-striped leaves, dense flower heads, 30cm (12in), flower stalks to 75cm (30in); *Helictotrichon sempervirens* (syn. *Avena candida*), grey-blue leaves, arching flower stalks, 1.2m (4ft); *Cortaderia selloana* (pampas grass; buy a named form as plants raised from seedlings don't flower reliably; at the end of the season pull out old foliage with strong gloves).
Varieties: 'Pumila', compact, flowers reliably, 1.75m (5ft 8in); 'Sunningdale Silver', sharp-edged leaves, cream flower heads, 1.5m (5ft), flower stalks to 2m (6½ft); *Elymus magellanicus*, silver-blue, 30cm (12in); *Festuca glauca*, steel blue, arching flower stalks, 25cm (10in), named forms such as 'Blaufuchs' are best; *Hakonechloa macra* 'Alboaurea', green and white-striped leaves, 35cm (14in); *Holcus mollis* 'Albovariegatus', silver-grey variegation, 25cm (10in); *Molinia caerulea* 'Variegata', green and yellow striped leaves, purple flower stalks, 60cm (24in); *Stipa arundinacea*, graceful, feathery flower heads, 75cm (30in); *Stipa gigantea*, green leaves, silvery flower heads, 45cm (18in), flower stalks to 2.5m (8ft).

Festuca glauca

Hedera

" The days have finally gone where ivies were thought of simply as boring evergreens. Many forms of H. helix are excellent container plants, their shade-tolerance and trailing evergreen habit being especially valuable for winter hanging baskets and window boxes. "

SPECIAL FEATURES

Many variegated ivies produce some all-green shoots, and these must be cut out promptly, otherwise they will gradually take over the entire plant.

SUITABLE CONTAINERS

Hanging baskets, window boxes, small tubs, large tubs. Vigorous forms must be planted in large tubs.
HEIGHT Most of those I recommend will trail to 1m (3ft).

Hedera helix **interplanted with** *Hosta aurea marginata*

RECOMMENDED VARIETIES

Non-vigorous forms of H. helix: 'Adam', small leaves with silver variegation; 'Brokamp', small leaves with green, yellow and white spots; 'Duckfoot', small green leaves with rounded lobes; 'Eva', small cream and green leaves; 'Glacier', green and silver-grey leaves 'Goldchild', gold leaves; 'Ivalace', small dark green leaves with turned up edges; 'Little Diamond', silver variegated leaves; 'Luzii', small leaves with green and gold marbling; 'Manda's Crested', pale green, wavy leaves; 'Parsley Crested' (syn. 'Cristata'), bright green leaves with crinkled edges; 'Très Coupé', tiny five-lobed green leaves.
Vigorous forms of H. helix: 'Goldheart' (syn. 'Oro di Bogliasco'), dark green leaves with a central gold blotch; 'Saggitifolia', five lobed leaves with slender points.

Helleborus

" I've often drawn comparisons between hellebores and euphorbias but, if I rarely see a euphorbia in a container, I very rarely see a hellebore. Yet, once again, there is no sound reason for this neglect, and hellebores' early spring flowering means that they can provide attractiveness and interest at a time when most other perennials have barely awoken from their winter rest. Also, hellebores provide an exception to the general rule that perennials raised from seed are inferior because they are extremely variable and there is always a good possibility of some attractive variants turning up. "

SPECIAL FEATURES

Cut back the browned foliage of *H. orientalis* in late winter, so that the emerging flower stems are shown to their best advantage.

SUITABLE CONTAINERS

Small tubs, large tubs.
HEIGHT 30–60cm (12–24in) – considerable variation in the species.

RECOMMENDED VARIETIES

H. argutifolius (syn. *H. corsicus*), coarsely toothed leaves, pale green, nodding flowers in spring; *H. foetidus*, pale green flowers with pink-purple tips in late winter and into spring, shade-tolerant, almost evergreen; *H. niger* (Christmas rose), white; the best form is the large-flowered 'Potter's Wheel', but all varieties should be given some protection from rain as the flowers open; *H. orientalis* (Lenten rose), colours range from white through pink, pale purple, mauve to deep purple, with many forms having variegated flower-colouring.

Hosta

" *Hostas are among the plants that every modern gardener is told they must have, for they are reckoned among the great perennials of the twentieth century. And yet anyone who ever grows them will discover that snails and slugs alike devour their foliage with evident relish. For this reason I no longer consider growing hostas anywhere other than in a container. I have two fine specimens in large pots in very prominent positions close to my garden pool.* "

SPECIAL FEATURES

I used to consider hosta flowers rather pathetic, but since then I've found that when the plant is allowed to become fairly pot-bound and is fed with a high-potash fertilizer, the flower spikes are much more impressive, and can add greatly to the attractiveness of the plant. They must be cut out as soon as the blooms fade, because otherwise the dying petals drop among the leaves and cause brown leaf spots to develop.

SUITABLE CONTAINERS

Small tubs, large tubs.

HEIGHT Varies from about 20cm (8in) to about 1m (3ft), depending on variety.

RECOMMENDED VARIETIES

This selection represents those I have used successfully in containers. H. 'August Moon', pale yellow, 60cm (24in) tall; H. crispula, dull green leaves with white edges, ribbed, wavy, 1m (3ft) tall; H. fortunei, steel blue, 75cm (30in) tall; H. albopicta, yellow and green streaks, 60cm (24in) tall; H. f. 'Francee', green leaves with white edge, 60cm (24in) tall; H. 'Gingko Craig', green leaves with white margin, 20cm (8in) tall; H. 'Krossa Regal', steel-blue with wavy leaf edge, 1m (3ft) tall; H. lancifolia, elongated leaves, green, 45cm (18in) tall; H. sieboldiana elegans, blue-green, 1m (3ft) tall; H. s. e. 'Frances Williams', steel blue, 1m (3ft) tall; H. undulata albomarginata (syn. 'Thomas Hogg'), green with cream edge, 60cm (24in) tall.

Hosta sieboldiana

Lamium

" *Lamiums, in common gardening language, are dead-nettles and, say many of my gardening friends, they are therefore no better than weeds. But to dismiss them in this way is to overlook some plants with quite remarkable foliage colours and, often, very pretty white, pink or yellow flowers on trailing stems that are just tailormade for hanging baskets.* "

SPECIAL FEATURES

As the flowers fade, lamiums will look untidy unless the old flower stems are cut back promptly; this also serves to encourage fresh new foliage to develop.

SUITABLE CONTAINERS

Hanging baskets, window boxes, small tubs.

HEIGHT Trailing to a length of about 60cm (24in).

RECOMMENDED VARIETIES

L. galeobdolon, pale yellow flowers; 'Florentinum' (syn. 'Variegatum'), silver-splashed leaves, turning purple in winter, upright habit, not for hanging baskets; L. g. 'Hermann's Pride', narrow leaves with silver streaks; L. g. 'Silberteppich' (syn. 'Silver Carpet'), striking silver leaves; L. maculatum 'Aureum', gold leaves, pink flowers; L. m. 'Beacon Silver', silver-white leaves, pink flowers; 'White Nancy', silver leaves with green margins and pretty, white flowers.

Lamium galeobdolon 'Florentinum'

Lysimachia

❝ *The genus* Lysimachia *is sometimes dismissed as the poor relation of the primula family, but I have always had a soft spot for its various species; both the tall border perennials and the species that concerns me here.* L. nummularia *is a native plant found along moist streamsides but its pretty flowers and creeping habit make it ideal for hanging baskets.* ❞

SPECIAL FEATURES

Its natural habitat is damp and slightly shady so, when growing it in a hanging basket, surround it with other larger-leaved plants to help keep it fresh.

Lysimachia nummularia 'Aurea'

RECOMMENDED VARIETIES
The normal species is the most common, but there is also a popular golden-leaved variant, 'Aurea'.

SUITABLE CONTAINERS
Hanging baskets.
HEIGHT Trails to about 45–50cm (18–20in).

Primula

❝ *Very few areas of the garden cannot be enhanced by one or other of the numerous species and varieties of* Primula, *arguably among the most valuable of all garden plant genera. Where containers are concerned, though, I would advise you to steer clear of the bog-garden types that require damp, slightly shady conditions and, indeed, to avoid all tall-stemmed forms because they really need the protection of other plants around them. The small alpine species will challenge the trough-garden specialist, but for more orthodox containers, you are likely to derive the most pleasure and satisfaction from the compact 'primrose' types which come in a wide range of colours.* ❞

SPECIAL FEATURES
Although primroses and some hybrids in mixed colours can be raised from seed, it is better if you grow the plants. Although many-coloured 'primrose' and 'polyanthus' types now almost rival universal pansies as winter bedding plants, they are less reliable in terms of tolerating the worst winter weather.

SUITABLE CONTAINERS
Window boxes, small tubs and large tubs.
HEIGHT 10–30cm (4–12in), depending on variety.

RECOMMENDED VARIETIES
Among the named forms you are likely to see are the true yellow primrose, *P. vulgaris* and the most popular of the *P. vulgaris* and *P. juliae* hybrids, the dark red-purple 'Wanda', but there are numerous other hybrids, generally unnamed and sometimes with huge flowers in shades of yellow, orange, purple, pink, red and white. Plants range in form from the primrose type, with short flower stems, to the 'polyanthus' type, which has numerous flowers atop a tall stem.

Primula vulgaris

Yucca gloriosa 'Variegata'

Yucca

❝ *Yuccas are among those plants about which I am still undecided. In their dominating spiky habit, they are unlike most other plants hardy enough to be grown outdoors and yet it is that very spikiness that is so difficult to blend with anything else. If you want to make a dominating feature in a formal courtyard, a yucca in an attractive pot will work like almost nothing else. But, whatever you do, don't put any other plants in the same container.* ❞

SPECIAL FEATURES

A number of species and varieties of *Yucca* are sold as indoor plants. These are not hardy enough to be used outdoors unless you are prepared to move what are inevitably large containers under cover in winter.

SUITABLE CONTAINERS
Large tubs.
HEIGHT 1–2m (3–6½ft).

RECOMMENDED VARIETIES
Y. filamentosa, whitish thread or filament-like edges to the leaves (the normal species has dark green leaves, 'Bright Edge' has yellow leaf margins, 'Variegata' has white or pinkish edges); *Y. gloriosa*, very sharply pointed (dangerously so) leaves, ('Variegata', with cream-and-yellow leaf stripes, is the best form); *Y. glauca*, glaucous leaves; *Y. flaccida* (syn. *Y. filifera*), very dark green leaves; *Y. recurvifolia*, upper leaves recurved. All may produce tall spikes of white or cream flowers, especially in warm seasons.

Vinca

❝ *The periwinkles are among the toughest of evergreen trailing plants, and provide valuable ground cover in the most inhospitable conditions. They are almost fully hardy and tolerate shade. This toughness has a particular value in containers, too. I have found no trailing plant more reliable in a winter hanging basket or any other winter container but you should use only the less vigorous species,* V. minor, *as other forms rapidly outgrow their containers.* ❞

SPECIAL FEATURES

To obtain the very best from your vincas you should use them in permanent plantings. The glossy, dark green foliage of *V. minor* will provide appeal during the winter, and then from mid-spring into summer, the very pretty white flowers are produced.

SUITABLE CONTAINERS
Window boxes, hanging baskets, small tubs, large tubs.
HEIGHT Trailing to a length of about 60cm–0.8m (24in–2½ft)

RECOMMENDED VARIETIES
All *V. minor*: *V. m.* species, green leaves, blue flowers; in the form 'Alba', green leaves, white flowers; 'Atropurpurea', green leaves, purple flowers; 'Aureovariegata', yellow and green leaves, blue flowers; 'Aureovariegata Alba', yellow and green leaves, white flowers.

BULBS

Bulbs almost beg to be grown in containers. They have a headstart in that the food reserve is within the bulb itself, and so flowering in the first year is virtually guaranteed. Moreover, spring-flowering types are especially valuable as they bring instant and glorious colour during those otherwise bleak weeks before the summer bedding can be planted. Some bulbs may be left permanently in their containers, but others are better lifted and then replanted the following season.

Agapanthus

" With the possible exception of lilies, I don't think any bulbous plant looks better in a container than a fine clump of Agapanthus. *But they aren't the hardiest of bulbs and, even where they will survive, they won't necessarily flower. As with everything in gardening, there will be exceptions that prove me wrong, but I wouldn't try* Agapanthus *in colder areas and they are undoubtedly at their best in mild places close to the sea. These large plants need plenty of space in which to display their charms.* "

SPECIAL FEATURES

Those species I recommend below are deciduous, and fare best if the containers are moved into a sheltered place in winter or, at least, the crowns are covered with a protective mulch.

SUITABLE CONTAINERS
Large tubs.
HEIGHT 1–1.5m (3–5ft).

RECOMMENDED VARIETIES
The most reliably successful are the 'Headbourne Hybrids', which include the full colour range, from dark blue-purple through to white.

Agapanthus '**Headbourne Hybrids**'

Allium karataviense

Allium

" A prophecy I made some years ago is at last coming true: alliums are beginning to be appreciated more widely as ornamental bulbs now that people have stopped thinking of them as merely flowering onions. Nonetheless, alliums have a good deal of catching up to do when it comes to people regarding them as spring or summer container plants. Choose your species carefully, as some have tall, slender stems that are vulnerable to damage unless there are other tall plants around them. "

SPECIAL FEATURES
The flower heads make excellent additions to dried arrangements.

SUITABLE CONTAINERS
Small tubs, large tubs.
HEIGHT Varies widely.

RECOMMENDED VARIETIES
A. *beesianum*, 25cm (10in), loose heads of bell-like blue flowers; A. *cyathophorum farreri*, 30cm (12in), loose heads each with a few red-purple flowers; A. *flavum*, 30cm (12in), loose heads each with numerous, bell-like yellow flowers; A. *karataviense*, 30cm (12in), spherical heads each with many small pink-purple flowers; A. *moly*, 30cm (12in), masses of small, star-like yellow flowers; A. *oreophilum*, 15cm (6in), loose heads of bell-like rose-pink flowers.

Anemone

" Anemone, like Iris, is a genus that spans a wide range of plant types, including fibrous-rooted border perennials as well as little bulbous rock-garden species. Aside from these alpine types, for example, A. nemorosa and A. blanda, which are often grown in trough gardens, anemones aren't seen very frequently in containers. Yet the large-flowered corm-forming hybrids in the A. coronaria group make excellent subjects for growing in small pots and popping into odd corners of the garden as they come into flower. "

SPECIAL FEATURES
These anemones aren't very reliable perennials; as the corms are relatively inexpensive, they are best grown as annuals. Stagger your planting times: plant up one pot every week or so for about six weeks in order to obtain continuity of flowering and interest.

SUITABLE CONTAINERS
Small tubs.
HEIGHT 30cm (12in).

RECOMMENDED VARIETIES
There are two widely available groups: 'St Brigid' and 'De Caen'. The former have semi-double flowers, the latter single. Both groups include white, red, pink, blue and mauve blooms, all of which are admirably set off by the deeply divided, almost ferny, foliage.

Anemone coronaria 'De Caen'

Crocus

" Crocuses are another example of a familiar, popular bulbous plant grown in most gardens but rarely seen in containers. I find the small-flowered varieties and species most appropriate for alpine troughs and similar plantings. For more general container use, I concentrate on the large-flowered Dutch crocus. "

SPECIAL FEATURES
I use large-flowered crocuses in containers in two ways: in small terracotta pots, planted with single colours, and dotted among other coloured spring flowers and for successional plantings in larger tubs. In mine, they appear in between the hyacinths and the tulips.

SUITABLE CONTAINERS
Small tubs, large tubs.
HEIGHT 15cm (6in).

RECOMMENDED VARIETIES
Most gardeners buy Dutch crocuses on the basis of colour alone, although the purity of the strains isn't reliable; you will often find one or two 'strangers' among the flowers when they appear. Look out especially for: 'Jeanne d'Arc', white with violet base; 'Purpureus Grandiflorus', deep purple; 'Golden Mammoth' (syn. 'Yellow Mammoth'), rich reddish-orange.

Cyclamen

❝ *Most cyclamen are grown in containers as the large-flowered varieties derived from* C. persicum *are among the most popular of house plants. Hardy cyclamens in containers are rarer, at least, outside the alpine garden. This must be because their flowers are small and, unless massed together, as in a garden bed, they make little impact. But I have found a way of growing small-flowered cyclamen in containers that is extremely effective and much-admired and this is in window boxes.* ❞

SUITABLE CONTAINERS
Window boxes, small tubs.
HEIGHT 10–15cm (4–6in).

SPECIAL FEATURES
The secret of success is two or three tubers in several 10cm (4in) diameter plant pots. The plants can live in these permanently, flower well and thrive on the lack of disturbance. As they come into flower each year, move the pots into the window box and pack a soil-free compost in between them.

RECOMMENDED VARIETIES
C. hederifolium, flowers in late summer and autumn, attractively marbled foliage (among the several named forms available is the white-flowered *C. h. albiflorum*); *C. coum*, flowers in late winter and spring, and has many selected foliage and flower variants.

Cyclamen coum

Galanthus Snowdrop

❝ *Snowdrops are not widely grown in containers for much the same reason, I suspect, as cyclamen: their flowers are so small that you need a great many to create an impact. There is another reason: snowdrops are best left undisturbed once they have settled into a flowering routine. Yet this need not militate against using them. Either grow them in window boxes, exactly as I suggest for cyclamen, or, because they are very much less costly, put masses in a large tub.* ❞

SPECIAL FEATURES
Always buy and plant snowdrops 'in the green'; that is, as growing plants after the flowers have faded. When planted as dry bulbs, snowdrops generally establish less satisfactorily, and flowering takes longer.

SUITABLE CONTAINERS
Window boxes, small/large tubs.
HEIGHT 15cm (6in). There are both taller- and shorter-growing snowdrop varieties available, but they are expensive.

RECOMMENDED VARIETIES
Of many named varieties of the common snowdrop, *G. nivalis*, the double-flowered 'Flore Pleno', is most frequently seen. For a really tall, majestic snowdrop, choose either *G. atkinsii* or *G.* 'S. Arnott'.

Hyacinthus
Hyacinth

❝ *Just as most cyclamens are grown in pots as house plants, so are most hyacinths. I'm sure that, proportionately, more hyacinths are also grown in outdoor containers, but still not as many as I would wish. It would upset me still further if I weren't greeted on spring mornings in my garden by the rich sweet fragrance drifting from the large tub of hyacinths that has been a feature close to the kitchen door for many years. Rather like daffodils (see page 65), hyacinths have the great merit among container plants in surviving very well from year to year as dried bulbs.* ❞

(see page 65)

SPECIAL FEATURES

Buy named varieties of hyacinths, and choose carefully which varieties you combine. The pinks are very assertive and really mix only with whites, unless you want a planting that looks like a christening cake. And nor do the various blues mix well with each other.

SUITABLE CONTAINERS
Window boxes, large tubs.
HEIGHT 20–25cm (8–10in).

RECOMMENDED VARIETIES
Varieties of *H. orientalis*: 'Anna Marie', pale pink; 'Delft Blue', pale blue; 'Jan Bos', red; 'White Pearl', white; 'Ostara', purple-blue; 'City of Haarlem', yellow.

Iris

❝ *Invaluable as irises are as garden plants, they don't have a great role to play in containers, with certain notable exceptions. The surface-rooting, border varieties do not succeed when confined, and the bog irises require wetter conditions than you can sensibly provide. The small, spring-flowering bulbous species, such as* I. reticulata *and* I. danfordiae, *may be grown as rock-garden plants in troughs. Grow Spanish, Dutch and English irises in containers only where it does not matter that they are in leaf longer than they are in flower. The one iris that I always grow in a container however is the glorious, winter-flowering variety* I. unguicularis. ❞

SPECIAL FEATURES

To obtain the most reliable flowering, plant the rhizomes in light, free-draining, soil-based compost, and place the pot in a sheltered, sunny spot in winter, and a hot, sunny spot in summer. The rhizomes must be *baked* to flower well.

SUITABLE CONTAINERS
Small tubs.
HEIGHT 20cm (8in).

RECOMMENDED VARIETIES
The normal species has pale lilac flowers but 'Mary Barnard', with deep blue-purple flowers, is much more imposing.

Hyacinthus 'Ostara'

Lilium Lily

66 *For me, lilies are the most wonderful of all bulbous plants to grow in containers. I say this not just because of their surpassing beauty and fragrance but also because, by growing them in containers, you can avoid most of the problems that arise when growing them in the open garden. Lilies are prey to millipedes, slugs and other soil inhabiting pests so, almost inevitably in the open garden, you will face fungal decay and poor performance. Glorious as they are in bloom, a faded lily is a sad and pathetic thing. How much more satisfactory it is when the lily (and its container) can be moved out of view to recharge its energies for the following year. Indeed, I now grow almost all of my lilies in containers and find that, by having a wide range of varieties, I can guarantee to have at least some in bloom from spring throughout summer.* 99

SPECIAL FEATURES

To keep lilies in top class condition you need to give just a little more than average care and attention. Be assiduous in giving liquid fertilizer after the flowers have faded, and be prompt in cutting or pulling away the dead stems. Mulch in early spring using leaf mould to which a handful of bonemeal has been added, and divide as infrequently as possible. Some varieties may need discrete staking, especially in windy situations but many lilies, though superficially fragile, are quite tough and wiry. The only real cloud on the lily-grower's horizon is the lily beetle, a bright red insect that is very difficult to control. Contact insecticides have limited effect; pick off and destroy the insects as soon as you see them.

Lilium 'Bright Star'

SUITABLE CONTAINERS

Large tubs, small tubs.
HEIGHT Varies with variety.

RECOMMENDED VARIETIES

Species: *L. candidum* (Madonna lily), 1.2m (4ft), early summer, white; *L. hansonii*, 1.2m (4ft), early summer, golden yellow with darker spots; *L. henryi*, 2m (6½ft), late summer, orange-yellow with darker spots; *L. martagon* (Turk's cap), 1.2m (4ft), summer, pale purple with darker spots; *L. monadelphum*, 1.5m (5ft), early summer, yellow with spotted throat; *L. regale*, 1m (3ft), summer, white with darker-streaked outsides, exquisite perfume, the finest of all lilies; *L. speciosum*, 1.2m (4ft), late summer, white with brown stamens (the best forms are the beautifully scented 'Album' and 'Ellabee').

Hybrids: 'Bright Star', 1m (3ft), summer, silver-white with a pale orange centre; 'Citronella' strain, 1.2m (4ft), summer, lemon yellow; 'Green Dragon', 1.5m (5ft), summer, white with a faint green flush outside, beautiful perfume; 'Orange Sensation' (a form of tiger lily), 1m (3ft), late summer, orange; 'Stargazer', 1.2m (4ft), late summer, red with pale margins.

Narcissus 'Tête-a-Tête'

Narcissus

All daffodils are narcissi but, strictly speaking, not many narcissi are daffodils. The genus Narcissus *is subdivided into about twelve categories, of which only those comprising plants with elongated trumpets are conventionally known as daffodils. Daffodils and narcissi are the most popular of all garden bulbs but not, for some reason, as container plants. I have never subscribed to this notion, so tubs of daffodils and narcissi are scattered around my garden every spring. Most of these plants are very easy to grow and practically all will be content in containers. By careful in your choice of varieties: plants can be in bloom from early spring almost into summer; longer still if you choose some dwarf species.*

SPECIAL FEATURES

You must buy named varieties, not mixtures; the latter will display a range of flowering times and, inevitably, the effect of the later-flowering types will be spoiled as they jostle with the dying blooms of the earlier varieties. Lift, carefully dry, and store the bulbs from your containers each year, and replace them with fresh stock if more than a quarter of the bulbs fail to flower.

SUITABLE CONTAINERS

Small tubs, large tubs.
HEIGHT Varies from around 20cm (8in) for the smaller species to 45cm (18in) for the most vigorous daffodils.

RECOMMENDED VARIETIES

Among true daffodils, the rich golden varieties tend to be among the earliest, and the whites among the latest to bloom.

Daffodils with small or large trumpets: 'Alliance', golden yellow; 'Arkle', golden yellow; 'Carlton', yellow; 'Dutch Master', golden yellow; 'Empress of Ireland', white; 'Fragrant Breeze', white with a pale yellow trumpet; 'Golden Aura', golden yellow; 'Golden Harvest', golden yellow; 'Ice Follies', white with a yellow interior to the trumpet; 'King Alfred', golden yellow; 'Mount Hood', white; 'Professor Einstein', white with an orange trumpet; 'Saint Keverne', yellow with a darker trumpet; 'Salmon Trout', white with a buff yellow trumpet; 'W. P. Milner', pale yellow.

Small-cupped narcissi: 'Barrett Browning', white with a flame-orange trumpet; 'Merlin', white with a yellow red-rimmed trumpet.

Double daffodils and narcissi: 'Acropolis', white with red centre; 'Cheerfulness', small, white with a yellow centre; 'Golden Ducat', yellow; 'Irene Copeland', white intermingled with pale orange; 'Petit Four', white with an apricot centre; 'Rip van Winkle', tiny, yellow with greenish edges; 'Unique', white with a yellow centre; 'Yellow Cheerfulness', yellow.

Triandrus and cyclamineus narcissi (with recurved or swept back petals): 'April Tears', golden yellow with a paler cup; 'Beryl', yellow with an orange cup; 'Charity May', yellow; 'Dove Wings', white with a yellow trumpet; 'February Gold', golden yellow with a darker cup; 'Hawera', yellow; 'Jack Snipe', white with a yellow cup; 'Jenny', white with a pale yellow cup; 'Liberty Bells', lemon-yellow; 'Little Witch', golden yellow; 'Peeping Tom', golden yellow; 'Rippling Waters', white; 'Tête-à-Tête', yellow with a golden yellow trumpet; 'Thalia', white.

Jonquils (two or more small, scented flowers per stem): 'Baby Moon', yellow; 'Bobbysoxer', yellow with a darker cup; 'Dickcissel', golden yellow; 'Suzy', yellow with an orange centre; 'Sweetness', yellow; 'Trevithian', yellow.

Tazettas (clusters of usually small, scented flowers): 'Geranium', white with a red-orange cup; 'Minnow', cream with a yellow cup.

Poeticus (small, flat, coloured cup with white petals): 'Cantabile', white with a greenish, red-edged cup.

Split corolla (orchid-flowered): 'Cassata', white with a yellow centre; 'Dolly Mollinger', white with an orange centre.

Species: *N. asturiensis*, golden yellow (a true miniature daffodil); *N. bulbocodium conspicuus*, golden yellow (a hoop petticoat daffodil); *N. poeticus recurvus* (old pheasant's eye), white with a yellow, red-edged cup; *N. pseudonarcissus* (Lent lily), yellow with a darker cup; *N. tazeta lacticolor*, white with a tiny yellow cup.

Nerine

  Gardeners may be divided into those who know and love nerines and those who don't. Clearly, those who don't know them won't grow them, but there is a rather large number of gardeners who have grown nerines and failed, and for this reason tend not to like them. This is rather sad, since the loose pink flower heads do have a special quality, matched only by some of the alliums (see page 60); with the difference that nerines are autumn-flowering. The real problem is that nerines must have a warm and sheltered spot and a well-drained soil. What better way to provide a well-drained soil and a warm and sheltered spot than by growing them in a container.

SPECIAL FEATURES

Apart from keeping them in too cold a place, the commonest reason for nerines to fail is their bulbs being planted in the same way as daffodils. Plant them more like shallots, with the tip of the bulb just appearing above the soil.

SUITABLE CONTAINERS
Small tubs.
HEIGHT 45–60cm (18in–24in).

RECOMMENDED VARIETIES:
There are several species and several varieties, some white-flowered but none are nearly as widely available or as pretty as the true species, *Nerine bowdenii*.

Nerine bowdenii

Scilla

  Just because bulbous plants are easy to grow successfully in the open ground doesn't mean you shouldn't grow them in containers. Yet I think this is what has happened with scillas (or spring squills, as the native species tend to be known). These absolutely charming little blue-flowered plants provide as cheerful a welcome as I know to the spring; why not let them play the same role in containers? However, they don't like being lifted, so containers should be dedicated to them and moved away for storage once flowering is over.

SPECIAL FEATURES

Allow the foliage to die down completely before pulling it away and give time for the seedheads to drop and disperse the seeds; the container will then fill up with plants far more quickly. Scillas are particularly useful in that they can tolerate light shade.

SUITABLE CONTAINERS
Small tubs.
HEIGHT 15cm (6in).

RECOMMENDED VARIETIES
S. mischtschenkoana (syn. *S. tubergeniana*), saucer-shaped pale blue; *S. siberica* 'Spring Beauty', brilliant sky blue, easily the finest of all scillas; *S. s.* 'Alba', white; a few intermingled with the blues can form a pleasing pattern.

Scilla mischtschenkoana

Tulipa 'Angelique'

Tulipa **Tulip**

❝ In recent years, I've tended to adopt the same approach to tulips as I have to lilies (see page 64); I grow most of them in containers. The reasons are much the same, in that I find they deteriorate and rot rapidly in open beds; even in my light, free-draining soil (on a heavy clay, the problems can be immeasurably worse). The difficulties are lesser with some, although by no means all, of the smaller-flowered species tulips, which will naturalize satisfactorily, but most of the large-flowered hybrids have to be grown more or less as annuals in the open garden. I'm sure this pleases the bulb trade, but it's jolly irritating to me. I find that, by using a good quality soil-based compost in containers, hybrid tulips will survive very much better and for several years, even without being lifted. ❞

SPECIAL FEATURES

The dying foliage on most tulips, especially the large-flowered hybrids, looks distinctly miserable and not something to be displayed in an ornamental pot. Yet, it must be allowed to die back fully if the bulbs are to retain their vigour for the following season. Whether the bulbs are to be left in the containers or lifted, it is sensible to move them swiftly out of view. I would emphasize that even if you do lift the bulbs you may find it rather late to put the containers to any other use since, by then, most of the summer plants and summer containers will have been planted.

Tulipa 'Red Riding Hood'

SUITABLE CONTAINERS
Large tubs, small tubs.
HEIGHT Varies with variety.

BULBS

Tulipa Tulip

RECOMMENDED VARIETIES

Species and near species:
T. acuminata, 45cm (18in), twisted green-and-red flowers; *T. biflora*, 15cm (6in), two tiny white flowers per stem; *T. clusiana*, 15cm (6in), cream-white with pale red streak; *T. humilis* (syn. *T. pulchella*) 'Violacea', 8cm (3½in), violet-purple with a black centre; *T. kaufmanniana*, 20cm (8in), white, yellow and pink; *T. kolpakowskiana*, 30cm (12in), yellow inside, red outside; *T. linifolia* 'Bronze Charm', 12cm (5in), apricot and bronze, exquisite; *T. linifolia* 'Maximowiczii', 15cm (6in), scarlet; *T.* 'Pinocchio', 20cm (8in), red-and-white striped; *T. praestans* 'Fusilier', 20cm (8in), three to five orange-red flowers per stem; *T.* 'Red Riding Hood' (illustrated on the previous page), 20cm (8in), red with a black base and mottled leaves; *T. saxatilis*, 30cm (12in), pink; *T.* 'Shakespeare', 20cm (8in), orange red; *T. sprengeri*, 35cm (14in), scarlet with bronze outside; *T. sylvestris*, 40cm (16in), yellow; *T. tarda*, 15cm (6in), white with a yellow centre (probably the easiest to naturalize); *T. turkestanica*, 20cm (8in), up to nine white, orange-centred flowers per stem; *T. urumiensis*, 15cm (6in), golden yellow and bronze; *T. orphanidia* 'Whittallii', 30cm (12in), bronze with deep-orange outside.
Large-flowered hybrids:
Early single: 'Bellona', gold; 'Keizerskroon', red with golden edges; 'Pink Beauty', pink with white stripe.
Early double: 'Peach Blossom', rose pink; 'Scarlet Cardinal', scarlet.
Mid-season, Triumph type: 'Athleet', white; 'Attila', deep purple; 'Garden Party', pink with white streak; 'New Design', pale-orange with red streaks; 'White Dream', white flowers.
Darwin hybrids (variably shaped single flowers, mid- to late-spring): 'Apeldoorn', scarlet; 'Elizabeth Arden', shades of pink; 'Golden Apeldoorn', golden yellow.
Single late: 'Clara Butt', pink; 'Queen of Night', dark-purple, nearly black.
Lily-flowered (narrow, waisted flowers): 'China Pink', pink; 'Marilyn', white with red streaks; 'White Triumphator', white; Viridiflora, some green colour in the petals; 'Artist', green, deep-pink and pale apricot; 'Groenland', green, cream and pink; 'Hollywood', green and crimson; 'Spring Green', shades of green, white and yellow; 'Parrot', single-flowers with frilled petals; 'Black Parrot', very dark-purple, nearly black; 'Blue Parrot', pale mauve; 'Flaming Parrot', golden yellow with red streaks; 'White Parrot', white.
Late double (peony-flowered): 'Angelique', pink and yellow; 'Gold Medal', golden yellow; 'Mount Tacoma', white; 'Maywonder', rich rose pink.

Zantedeschia

❝ Zantedeschias seem to have several quite different groups of devotees. Water-garden enthusiasts appreciate their white arum-like spathes and grow them as marginal plants at the pool edge (see Best Water Plants*). Flower arrangers are entranced by the exotic and extravagantly coloured tender varieties grown indoors. In between is perhaps the smallest group: gardeners who grow zantedeschias outdoors in containers for summer ornamentation but then move them under cover for winter protection. I hope that this group will become far larger. Some form of frost-free protection is essential if these plants are not to succumb. ❞*

SPECIAL FEATURES
Zantedeschias are naturally plants which prefer damp and often lightly shaded places. They must have a rich, organic moisture-retentive compost, and should be watered regularly.

SUITABLE CONTAINERS
Small tubs.
HEIGHT 30–45cm (12–18in).

RECOMMENDED VARIETIES
The normal species, green leaves and a white spathe; 'Crowborough', similar but slightly more vigorous and hardy; 'Green Goddess', striking but slightly less hardy, cream-white spathe with green margins.

ROSES

I could no more garden without roses than I could garden without soil. (I discuss the invaluable role these plants play in garden planning and design in Book 7 of this series, *Best Roses*). But there is one area where roses can be more difficult: in container gardening. There are two main reasons for this. Any plant with some deep major roots and comparitively few fibrous surface roots will need a relatively deep container. Similarly, any plant which requires a moisture-retentive soil is unlikely to be very happy in a free-draining potting compost that may be watered infrequently. Nonetheless, all plants can be grown in containers, and there are times when it is advantageous to do so with roses: in very small courtyard gardens with almost no open-bed spaces; beside walls where a climber is needed, but where it is quite impossible to create an open planting position because the ground is made of concrete or another hard material; and when there is a need, which wouldn't be satisfied by a raised bed, for an elevated feature in a flat planting area.

Because the requirements, both aesthetic and functional, vary between the main types of roses, I consider each separately although there are a few general points. Use John Innes No 3 Soil-based Potting Compost but, before planting, add half by volume of organic matter. Be assiduous in feeding, watering and mulching; the effects of neglect will be magnified in a container. Prune exactly as you would if the roses were in the open garden. In my descriptions on these pages, rather than recommend individually named roses, I have indicated groups. For more precise recommendations within each group, your best plan is to turn to *Best Roses*.

Miniatures and Patio Roses

SPECIAL FEATURES
The Miniatures are usually smaller than the Patio Roses (which are really dwarf Floribundas) but, in fact, the term 'Miniature' really applies to their flowers, which are tiny.

Rosa 'Tear Drop'

SUITABLE CONTAINERS
Small tubs.
HEIGHT Ranges up to about 45cm (18in).

RECOMMENDED VARIETIES
Any; this is the best group for container growing and, even though I have room in my garden, I grow all of my Miniature varieties in containers; as much as anything because I find their slightly more tender nature is better protected this way.

Climbing and Rambling Roses

SPECIAL FEATURES
My advice is to choose a variety that is of the minimum vigour needed to cover its allotted space. I would never use a container for a variety that reaches more than about 4m (13ft).

SUITABLE CONTAINERS
Large tubs.
HEIGHT Ranges from around 2m (6½ft) for short climbers which overlap in size with medium-sized shrubs, to 10m (33ft) or over for the more vigorous species.

RECOMMENDED VARIETIES
Climbing forms of Hybrid Teas and Floribundas; the shorter-growing Modern Climbers; climbing Miniatures: but not Ramblers, Climbing species or climbing forms of most Old Shrub varieties, although the few surviving Climbing Tea Roses work well. The climbing rose group (particularly very vigorous varieties) will present the greatest problems, as the root system will be extensive, and the top growth of the plants will be large.

ROSES

Modern Bush Roses (Floribundas & Hybrid Teas)

SPECIAL FEATURES

Unlike most Shrub Roses, and certainly most Old Shrub Roses, these Modern Bush varieties have the virtue of flowering throughout the summer months, either intermittently, or more or less continuously and so have a very special merit, particularly in small gardens or courtyards.

SUITABLE CONTAINERS
Large tubs.
HEIGHT Ranges from about 45–1.2m (18in–4ft), occasionally reaches more.

Rose 'Fritz Nobis'

RECOMMENDED VARIETIES

Any except the very largest and most vigorous.

Standard Roses

SPECIAL FEATURES

Standard Roses are roses in small-tree form, produced by budding (or grafting) the flowering variety atop a single upright stem. Any flowering variety can be used although the ones generally employed are usually Hybrid Teas or Floribundas. Rambling or spreading Shrub Roses are sometimes used to produce Weeping Standards.

SUITABLE CONTAINERS
Large tubs for Standards and small tubs for Half- and Quarter-standards.
HEIGHT The traditional Standard has the flowering variety budded at a height of about 1m (3ft), while Half-standards are budded at about 0.8m (2½ft) and Quarter-standards at 45cm (18in).

Rose 'The Fairy'

RECOMMENDED VARIETIES

Almost any, although full-sized Weeping Standards can become very big and look distinctly unwieldy in a container.

Shrub Roses

SPECIAL FEATURES

Do not select varieties that will grow to much more than 1.5m (5ft) for container use. Choose roses whose habit is compact and upright rather then open and spreading.

Rosa 'Nozomi'

SUITABLE CONTAINERS
Large tubs.
HEIGHT Ranges from about 1.2m (4ft) up to 2.5m (8ft).

RECOMMENDED VARIETIES

Among the best shrub roses for containers are the lower-growing Modern Shrubs, the English Roses, most of the Rugosas, the Gallicas, some of the Centifolias and the Moss Roses. By and large you should avoid the species and near-species, the Damasks, Albas, Chinas, Bourbons and Hybrid Perpetuals, all of which tend to be too large and cumbersome for container planting.

SHRUBS

I believe shrubs are the most important plants in the modern garden; they offer so much visiual appeal in return for so little effort. And, shrubs in containers are of particular value in small gardens where a conventional shrub border would not be possible. Do weigh up the year-round merits carefully before choosing any particular variety; although an evergreen might seem the best bet, few evergreens have spectacular flowers, whereas deciduous shrubs can offer summer flowers, autumn leaf colour and attractive winter bark.

Aucuba

❝ Aucuba, *the spotted laurel, is one of the most versatile shrubs and one of the easiest to grow – so easy, indeed, it is almost maligned on this count. Its supreme virtue, the toleration of both shade and dryness, is of particular value for the container gardener, especially if you have only a small, rather shaded area in which to place your containers. And, common or not, I still consider* Aucuba *a very pretty plant with its variously spotted fresh green leaves and, if you choose a female form, its rich red berries.* ❞

SUITABLE CONTAINERS
Large tubs.
HEIGHT Up to about 4m (13ft).

RECOMMENDED VARIETIES
A. japonica: 'Crotonifolia', female, small leaf spots, some all-yellow leaves, prone to shoot-blackening; 'Gold Dust', female, sparse yellow-gold spots; 'Picturata', male, dark green-yellow blotched leaves; 'Rozannie', hermaphrodite, sparse berries, all-green leaves; 'Salicifolia', female, elongated all-green leaves.

Aucuba japonica **'Picturata'**

Buddleja

❝ *I considered* Buddleja *too vigorous for containers until I tried that glorious, but rather tender hybrid,* B. x lewisiana *'Margaret Pike'. The only sufficiently sheltered spot in my garden offered no bare soil, so into a rather small pot she went. And there she has stayed, even through some cold winters, growing and blooming splendidly. Since then I've grown various forms of* B. davidii *very successfully in pots.* ❞

SPECIAL FEATURES
Cut back all shoots on late-flowering forms to about 15cm (6in) above compost level in mid- to late spring.

SUITABLE CONTAINERS
Large tubs.
HEIGHT Varies with species; B. davidii, pruned annually reaches about 2m (6½ft) in a container; other species about 15m (50ft), ultimately.

RECOMMENDED VARIETIES
B. alternifolia, early summer-flowering cascades of honey-scented lilac flowers; B. davidii, late summer-flowering, matchless for attracting butterflies; 'Black Knight', dark purple; 'Dartmoor', magenta; 'Empire Blue', blue-mauve with orange eye; 'Nanho Blue', pale blue; 'Royal Red', deep red-purple; 'White Bouquet', white with yellow centre; B. fallowiana alba, white with orange eye; B. 'Lochinch', blue-mauve.

Buxus Box

❝ *Box is second only to yew as a neat evergreen hedging and topiary plant, even if the topiary is no more extravagant than a carefully clipped and shaped sphere. So popular has topiary become, even in small gardens, that many people grow the plants in containers and this is an excellent and versatile way of doing it.* ❞

SPECIAL FEATURES

Box is valuably tolerant of moderate or almost deep shade, and is best clipped twice: once in mid-summer and once in early autumn.

Buxus sempervirens ‘Suffruticosa’

SUITABLE CONTAINERS
Small tubs, large tubs.
HEIGHT Clipped regularly, box will put on only a few centimetres in height per year.

RECOMMENDED VARIETIES
The best and most widely available box for topiary is *B. sempervirens* although there are also many variants. Among the all-green forms, I like ‘Angustifolia’ (syn. ‘Longifolia’); if you need a neat, very slow growing form, use ‘Suffruticosa’. Among the best variegated forms are: ‘Aureovariegata’, rounded leaves with gold edges and small blotches; ‘Elegantissima’, small leaves with white edges; and ‘Latifolia Maculata’, very dark green leaves with yellow-gold blotches, especially towards the shoot-tips.

Camellia

❝ *There are few sights in the garden more splendid than a well grown camellia flowering in a fine terracotta pot. It is also the classic example of a plant with rather specific soil requirements and so, in many gardens, they can only be grown in a container of appropriate compost. So fine are they that if I had to choose a plant to grace the very best container that I could afford, I think it would have to be a camellia.* ❞

SPECIAL FEATURES

Camellias must be grown in an acidic compost; the best currently available are peat-based . Place the containers in a slightly shaded and sheltered position. No pruning should be needed other than the occasional cutting out of wayward shoots, ideally after flowering.

Camellia x *williamsii* ‘Donation’

SUITABLE CONTAINERS
Small tubs, large tubs.
HEIGHT Some variation between species and varieties; most of the camellias mentioned below will slowly reach about 2.5–3 m (8–10ft).

RECOMMENDED VARIETIES
Hybrids of the C. x *williamsii* group: ‘Anticipation’, deep pink, paeony-flowered, very floriferous; ‘Brigadoon’, silvery-pink, large double; ‘Donation’, pink, large, semi-double (very reliable); ‘E G Waterhouse’, pink, double; ‘Elsie Jury’, pink, large anemone or paeony-flowered; ‘Saint Ewe’, pink, large, cup-shaped, single.
Other hybrids: ‘Inspiration’, deep pink, semi-double; ‘Leonard Messel’, deep pink, loosely double.

Clematis

" *For many years I considered that* Clematis, *like most other perennial climbers, wasn't really successful in containers for all of the usual reasons: the plants are deep-rooted, the compost can't be kept sufficiently and uniformly moist, and so forth. And then, at one of the big garden shows I saw some exhibited by a specialist* Clematis *nursery that were among the finest I have seen anywhere. Since then, I have grown them very successfully myself although it is still important to avoid the most vigorous species.* "

SPECIAL FEATURES

Shade the container so that the roots are kept cool and mulch the compost early in the season. I describe pruning in Book 1 of this series, *Best Climbers*: basically, prune all in spring and remember, the later in the season the variety flowers, the harder it should be pruned.

SUITABLE CONTAINERS

Large tubs.
HEIGHT Varies considerably; for container growing select those that don't exceed about 2–3m (6½–10ft).

RECOMMENDED VARIETIES

There are vast numbers of *Clematis* varieties and my recommendations are given in *Best Clematis*. For containers, my advice is simply to try any except the vigorous *C. montana* and its varieties/related species.

Clematis macropetala **'Maidwell Hall'**

Cytisus Broom

" Cytisus *is a small but varied genus of shrubs which includes both deciduous and a few evergreen species. They are versatile plants, tolerant, although never really successful in the cold and wet. Cytisus bloom mainly in the spring and early summer, bearing masses of small, pea-like flowers. The low-growing forms look splendid cascading from a tub; or try the small tree-sized* C. battandieri. "

SPECIAL FEATURES

The plants fare very much better if you feed them. With the exception of *C. battandieri*, they resent pruning.

SUITABLE CONTAINERS

Small tubs (for the prostrate species), large tubs.
HEIGHT Prostrate forms create mounds of growth about 30cm (12in) high; in a container *C. battandieri* can attain 4m (13ft).

RECOMMENDED VARIETIES

C. x *beanii*, yellow flowers, forms a low mound; *C.* x *kewensis*, cream-white flowers, creeping habit; *C. battandieri*, small tree-sized with grey-green leaves and masses of yellow, pineapple-scented flowers.

SHRUBS

Fatsia

❝ *Fatsias always look like house plants and so they continue to surprise the unenlightened with their hardiness. In fact they are invaluable container plants simply because of one special property; there are few other hardy evergreens with such large and glossy foliage. That is not to say that they will survive in the very coldest gardens nor that they are right in every situation. Their special, exotic features look best in enclosed courtyards (or 'outdoor rooms') and then they are splendid with other container-grown foliage such as hardy ferns.* ❞

SPECIAL FEATURES
Fatsias won't tolerate full sun so position them with this in mind.

SUITABLE CONTAINERS
Small tubs, large tubs.
HEIGHT Will ultimately reach about 4m (13ft), but can be easily restricted by pruning.

RECOMMENDED VARIETIES
The choice lies between the normal glossy-leaved dark green species and 'Variegata' which has leaves with cream tips.

Hamamelis mollis

Fatsia japonica **'Variegata'**

Hamamelis Witch hazel

❝ *The witch hazels are expensive plants to buy; largely because they are slow-growing and need to be grafted. They are also slightly tender and intolerant of heavy, impoverished or alkaline soils. Yet, as early-spring flowering deciduous shrubs, they have few rivals. Because of their rather exacting site requirements, they make wonderful container plants. The fragrant flowers which appear as little spidery tufts on the bare twigs are indeed striking. Most forms also display rich autumn colours, especially when in a fairly acidic compost. Because of the greyness of the bark, I find they look much better in stone or, if you can manage it, lead containers rather than terracotta ones.* ❞

SPECIAL FEATURES
Witch hazels don't need pruning and, in fact, tend to react rather badly to it. I have known several cases where owners unwisely thought they could shape the plants, only to discover that a combination of coral spot-disease and general resentment resulted in the plant's untimely demise.

SUITABLE CONTAINERS
Large tubs.
HEIGHT Given good conditions *Hamamelis* plants will become small trees up to 5m (16ft) tall but they are very slow growing and, in a container, they will normally not exceed 2m (6½ft).

RECOMMENDED VARIETIES
There are three common species, two Oriental and one North American. The most popular and widely available is the hybrid between the two Oriental species, *H. mollis* and *H. japonica* known as *H. x intermedia*, especially in its fine sulphur-yellow flowered form, 'Pallida'; other attractive varieties of the same plant are: 'Arnold Promise', deep yellow; 'Diane', rich red; 'Jelena', yellow with a reddish flush. *H. mollis* itself is a fine plant with fragrant, rich yellow flowers, reddish at the base.

Hydrangea

" *The genus* Hydrangea *means different things to different people. To many gardeners, especially those who garden in mild areas close to the sea, the large blue- or pink-flowered mop-headed forms of* H. macrophylla *are perhaps the commonest of all shrubs. The woodland gardener, however, will grow a whole range of other generally white-flowered species. In between are the glorious lace-caps with their delicate traceries of* white or mauve flowers. All are good plants and all can be grown in containers provided you bear two things in mind: grow hydrangeas in containers only if they grow satisfactorily in your area in the open ground (for the ability to grow them depends more on climate than on soil), and don't forget that they are all intolerant of dry conditions so you must pay special attention to watering.* "

SUITABLE CONTAINERS

Large tubs.
HEIGHT Varies between species but most will ultimately attain about 3m (10ft).

SPECIAL FEATURES

Provide protection for the crowns in winter by mounding compost around them. Prune the mop-headed and lace-cap forms of *H. macrophylla* in spring by cutting back the oldest one-third of the shoots to a bud close to the base. Then take off the dead flower heads on the remainder (do *not* remove these in the autumn) to a strong pair of leaves about one-third of the way down the shoot. Other types require no pruning.

On alkaline composts, you can enhance the blue colour of *H. macrophylla* by applying proprietary blueing powder (aluminium sulphate) to the compost. Unfortunately, most of the acidic composts are not satisfactory if you want a long-term plant.

RECOMMENDED VARIETIES

(Alternative colours in alkaline/acid conditions given if appropriate.)
H. macrophylla (mop-headed types): 'Ami Pasquier', red/purple; 'Ayesha', pink/lilac; 'Blauer Prinz' (syn. 'Blue Prince'), deep pink/clear blue; 'Generale Vicomtesse de Vibraye', pink/clear blue; 'Madame Emile Mouilliere', white or pale pink/white; *H. macrophylla* (lace-cap types): 'Lanarth White', pink/blue with outer florets almost always white; 'Mariesii Perfecta' (syn. 'Blue Wave), pink/electric blue. Others: *H. aspera*, pink-lilac ray florets, the most glorious of the lace-caps (the form called 'Villosa' or *H. villosa* is widely available); *H. involucrata* 'Hortensis', small double pink-white flowers; *H. paniculata*, elongated, fluffy white flower heads, glorious (but choose 'Grandiflora'); *H. serrata*, flowers in large flattish or slightly rounded clusters; choose 'Blue Bird', pink/blue, or 'Grayswood', pale pink/pink; *H*. 'Preziosa' pink/pink.

Hydrangea **'Madame Emile Mouilliere'**

Lavandula   Lavender

❝ *Until a few years ago, I wouldn't have thought of growing lavender in pots. I was converted, however, by a display I saw in France of* Lavandula stoechas *(the so-called French lavender) as the centre-piece of a fine herb garden. I felt that anything the French can do with French lavender, I can do with English; and so I did. There are so many places in the garden where lavender can be used: in a herb garden, of course, as I first saw it, but it can also be a readily portable part of a traditional cottage garden. Have one or two pots of lavender and then, as they come into flower, pop them among other plants already in bloom; they look wonderful among a bed of pot marigolds.* ❞

SPECIAL FEATURES
As the flowers fade, clip fairly hard to encourage fresh growth; otherwise the plants will become straggly and woody.

RECOMMENDED VARIETIES
Varieties of *L. angustifolia* (also called *L. officinalis* or *L. spica*, Old English lavender): 'Alba', white; 'Hidcote', deep violet-blue; 'Loddon Pink', pink-blue with long flower stalks; 'Munstead', lavender blue; 'Rosea', pink-blue, compact; 'Twickel Purple', rich purple, a neat bushy plant.
Others: *L x intermedia* 'Grappenhall', lilac; *L. stoechas* (French lavender), evergreen, dark purple, curious flask-like flower heads; move containers under cover in winter.

Lavandula stoechas

SUITABLE CONTAINERS
Small tubs, large tubs.
HEIGHT Most lavenders reach about 60cm (24in); a few selections can attain as much as 1m (3ft).

Potentilla

❝ *Time and again, when I'm asked for suggestions of small flowering shrubs suitable for a sunny spot and with a long season, I find myself suggesting potentillas. And just as I recommend them for the open garden, so too for containers. Indeed, provided they aren't allowed to dry out, I can think of few better small and easy-to-grow shrubs. There are many varieties in a considerable range of sizes yet some of the newer ones have disappointing colours. But the ones I suggest below have never disappointed me.* ❞

SPECIAL FEATURES
Don't be tempted to prune potentillas in the early spring, thinking they have died back; they always look like that.

Potentilla fruticosa 'Primrose Beauty'

RECOMMENDED VARIETIES
Varieties of *P. fruticosa*: 'Daydawn', pink-peach; 'Goldfinger', golden yellow (a larger, more vigorous plant with fine flowers, worth occasional pruning after flowering if it threatens to become too big); 'Manchu', white, almost prostrate, one of my great favourites – lovely cascading from a pot; 'Primrose Beauty', clear primrose-yellow; 'Tilford Cream', cream-white.

SUITABLE CONTAINERS
Small tubs, large tubs.
HEIGHT Those I recommend will reach about 60cm–1m (24in–3ft).

Philadelphus

❝ Unless you have a very large conservatory or, better still, an orangery for winter protection, you won't grow oranges in containers very readily outdoors. But if I can't offer you the fruit, at least I can offer you the rich, sweet fragrance of orange blossom. Although you can obtain this fragrance from a number of shrubs, you will achieve it best of all with the true mock oranges (if that isn't a contradiction) of the genus Philadelphus. Many people will be familiar with these as garden plants and will be aware that they can grow very large; but let me introduce some smaller varieties that I have grown with great success in tubs and which will create the most deliciously heady fragrance, especially in a confined area. ❞

SPECIAL FEATURES
If the mock oranges have any drawback, it is that most have a rather stiff, stark twiggy appearance in the winter; but the same could be said of many other shrubs, and the heavenly summer perfume is admirable compensation.

SUITABLE CONTAINERS
Large tubs.
HEIGHT Those I recommend below shouldn't exceed about 2m (6½ft) in a container.

RECOMMENDED VARIETIES
'Beauclerk', single white with a pinkish centre; 'Belle Etoile', single white with a dark purple central spot; 'Manteau d'Hermine', double white.

Philadelphus **'Belle Etoile'**

Philadelphus **'Beauclerk'**

Rhododendron (and Azalea)

" *Of all the shrubs that are grown in gardens with soil unsuited to them, rhododendrons must top the list. Too often one sees plants grown in the open ground suffering dreadfully because of the alkalinity, and yet plants grown in containers of acidic compost usually look splendid. Yes, there's undoubtedly something about rhododendrons that holds a magnetic attraction for most gardeners, while having quite the reverse effect on a few. I confess I'm in the former category and yet I have never had a garden with an acidic soil, so all of my rhododendron growing has been in small peat beds or containers. Bear two things in mind: don't be over-ambitious (restrict yourself to the smaller-growing varieties), and remember that while rhododendrons fare best in light shade, their close relatives, azaleas, are best in sun.* "

SPECIAL FEATURES

Use an acidic compost. Plant with the roots just below the surface, mulch in spring and apply sequestered iron. Don't prune unless the plants become severely misshapen.

SUITABLE CONTAINERS

Large tubs.

HEIGHT Varies enormously from dwarf alpines to trees (see adjacent) so choose carefully.

Rhododendron 'Razorbill'

RECOMMENDED VARIETIES

The following very limited selection is essentially of small, hardy and reliable forms, taken from the most widely available types and based on those of which I have some experience.

True rhododendrons: (unless stated, all growing to about 1m (3ft) tall): *R. impeditum*, dwarf, mauve blue; *R. pemakoense*, bell-shaped, lilac-purple; *R. williamsianum*, bell-shaped, pink; *R. yakushimanum*, bell-shaped, rose pink buds, opening pink-white (a magnificent small shrub, expensive but far superior to the hybrids derived from it); 'Blue Tit', lavender blue; 'Bow Bells', loose, bell-shaped, pink; 'Carmen', dark red; 'Chikor', dwarf, yellow; 'Dora Amateis', white; 'Elizabeth', dark red, 1.5m (5ft) tall; 'Humming-bird', bell-shaped, scarlet; 'Razorbill', vivid pink; 'Snipe', pink.

Azalea hybrids (all evergreens growing to about 1m (3ft) tall): 'Addy Wery', dark red; 'Blaauw's pink'; 'Blue Danube', mauve-blue; 'Hinode-giri', crimson; 'Hino-mayo', pink; 'Kure-no-yuki', white; 'Mother's Day', red; 'Orange Beauty'; 'Vuyk's Scarlet'.

Deciduous azalea hybrids (all growing to 2–2.5m (6½–8ft) tall): 'Berryrose', pink-flushed yellow; 'Cecile', salmon pink; 'Gibralter', orange-flushed yellow; 'Homebush', pink; 'Persil', white-flushed orange; 'Strawberry Ice', pink with yellow flush.

Viburnum

" *Viburnum is a big genus containing a large number of both deciduous and evergreen species some of which have a wonderful winter and early spring flowers. Few gardens would not be enhanced by one or other species, yet viburnums remain the unsung heroes of the shrubbery. Perhaps this is because none are out-and-out show-offs; and maybe it is for this same reason that they are so seldom seen in containers. Yet these are plants which have a great deal to offer. While most viburnums are undeniably on the large side, I have grown several in containers extremely successfully, limiting the size by careful pruning when it becomes neccessary.* "

RECOMMENDED VARIETIES

For winter or early spring flowers: *V.* x *burkwoodii*, masses of fragrant white flowers, semi-evergreen; *V.* x *carlcephalum*, similar to *V.* x *burkwoodii* but deciduous; *V. carlesii*, strongly and sweetly scented white flowers, rounded grey-green leaves with felted undersides, deciduous with good autumn colour. There are many inferior forms but 'Aurora' is good.
Evergreen foliage types: *V. davidii*, elongated, rather matt green leaves and clusters of tiny, elongated dark blue fruits in autumn, unisexual, so both male and female clones are needed.

SPECIAL FEATURES

Viburnums are particularly valuable in lightly shaded spots; they seldom give of their best in full sun. By choosing carefully from the wide range of deciduous and evergreen forms, it's possible to have considerable variety in leaf form and degree of glossiness as well as in the shape and colour of the fruits.

SUITABLE CONTAINERS
Large tubs.
HEIGHT Those I recommend below will gradually attain about 1.5m (5ft), limited by pruning.

Virburnum davidii

Viburnum x carlcephalum

Much the same remarks apply to trees in containers as to shrubs (see page 74): it is very important to choose one that will offer some interest all year round. Because of its overall form, a tree in a container is likely to be an important focal point and the tracery of bare winter branches of a deciduous species can perform this role more effectively than the unchanging dispay of an evergreen.

Acer

❝ There can be few trees that produce more gasps of delight and admiration than an acer in autumn. It's no surprise that people want to have one in their gardens; but therein lies the difficulty. The best acers for autumn leaf-colour in this country are among the Asiatic types; the American species don't perform as well as they do in their homeland. It appears to be the predictable combination of warm days and cold nights in early autumn that we seem to lack. But most of the best of the Asiatic maples are highly intolerant of cold winds, exposure and waterlogging. What better excuse can there be for growing one of the dwarf or very slow-growing forms in an attractive container in a sheltered spot? Do remember, however, that it may be unwise to choose a plant solely on the basis of its appearance for two or three weeks of the year. Having attractive foliage for the remaining fifty or so weeks is very important, too, and while the overall impact of a tree with unfurling leaves and opening blossom in spring is a delightful sight, in most species the flowers are predominantly greenish and individually rather uninteresting. ❞

SPECIAL FEATURES

If the containers are small enough to be moved, there is much to be said for taking the plants into a more sheltered position in winter; and certainly if your garden is exposed.

SUITABLE CONTAINERS

Large tubs.

HEIGHT Varies with type. Avoid fast growing species and those, such as the Norway maple, that eventually become very large.

Acer palmatum

RECOMMENDED VARIETIES

Three Oriental species, *Acer japonicum*, *A. palmatum* and *A. shirasawanum* offer much the best choices, with many different leaf shapes and varying intensity of autumn colour. The named forms are invariably sold as grafted plants and largely because of this, are often expensive.

The following are among the most widely available and reliable in my experience.

Forms of *A. shirasawanum* (which may be listed under *Acer japonicum*): *A. s.* 'Aureum', pale green in spring, yellow in summer, red-orange in autumn, height 2m (6½ft) after ten years, 3m (10ft) ultimately (in the right spot, a glorious plant).

Forms of *A. palmatum*: normal species, palm-shaped green leaves, red in autumn; *A. p. atropurpureum*, palm-shaped deep-purple leaves, red and scarlet in autumn; *A. p.* 'Osakazuki', seven-lobed olive green leaves, vivid red autumn colour, height 3m (10ft) after ten years, 5m (16ft) ultimately; *A. p. dissectum*, finely divided, ferny green leaves, red-orange in autumn; *A. p. d.* 'Dissectum Atropurpureum' and 'Garnet', similar to *A. p. dissectum* but with deep-purple leaves, changing to red-orange in autumn, height 1.2m (4ft) after ten years, 1.5m (5ft) ultimately.

Forms of *A. japonicum*: 'Aconitifolium', very finely divided nine- or eleven-lobed leaves, rich green, purple in autumn, height slowly reaches 3m (10ft).

Acer japonicum **'Aureum'**

Amelanchier

Amelanchier lamarckii

  " At the risk of being boring, I shall repeat what I have said on many other occasions: this is **the** perfect small garden tree. It tolerates a wide range of soils (including clay) and a wide range of climatic conditions (including strong wind). It offers something at all seasons, with delicate white blossom appearing in spring, just as the dainty, elliptical leaves unfurl. These leaves turn vivid red in autumn when they are accompanied by dark red berries; provided the weather is warm and the birds sparse. In winter, a tracery of fine twigs continues the interest. I have grown an amelanchier in every one of the gardens I have owned, and it was almost certainly the first tree that I planted in my present garden. I'd like to think I've done my bit to ensure that many gardens are now equally blessed. But how often do you see an amelanchier in a container? Not very often, so perhaps that should be my second crusade. **"**

SPECIAL FEATURES

Not least among the choice features of amelanchiers is that they require no pruning, although they do respond favourably to a little shaping.

SUITABLE CONTAINERS
Large tubs.
HEIGHT 3–4m (10–13ft) after ten years, 5–6m (16½–20ft) ultimately; it is often said to grow considerably taller, but in my experience it doesn't do so in gardens.

RECOMMENDED VARIETIES

There are several closely related species of which A. *lamarckii* is the one to choose. A. *canadensis* and A. 'Ballerina' are inferior.

Magnolia

66 *Magnolias are good for growing in larger containers provided you avoid the more vigorous species, as they don't respond well to pruning and, therefore, can't easily be restricted in size. The recommended forms are hardy, although frost can damage the blossom.* 99

SPECIAL FEATURES

If the plants threaten to outgrow their container, the trick is to grow them 'confined' for three or four years then plant them out in the open garden.

SUITABLE CONTAINERS
Large tubs.
HEIGHT Varies. Heights given here are after ten years.

RECOMMENDED VARIETIES
M. liliiflora, tulip-shaped flowers in late spring (the commonest form is 'Nigra'), 2m (6½ft) tall; *Magnolia* x *loebneri*, star-like spring flowers at an early age (among the best forms are 'Leonard Messel' with pink-mauve flowers and 'Merrill' with white flowers), 6m (20ft) tall; *M.* x *soulangeana*, tulip-shaped flowers in spring ('Alba Superba', white flowers with purple bases and 'Lennei', flowers with rose-purple outsides and cream within), 4m (13ft) tall; *M. stellata*, star-like spring flowers ('Royal Star', white flowers and 'King Rose', pink flowers), perhaps the best magnolia for a container, 1.5m (5ft) tall.

Magnolia liliiflora

Malus Crab apple

66 *Predictably, since apples are their close relatives, the ornamental forms of* Malus *have an advantage over all other blossom trees as container plants: they are all available grafted, at least to special order, onto a dwarfing rootstock. The rootstock M.27 is the* one to choose, and is itself ideally suited to the good compost and general growing conditions that a container offers. My specimen of 'John Downie' has been in a large tub for ten years and delights me every year with both its blossom and its fruits.* 99

SPECIAL FEATURES

Ornamental crab apples are subject to the same pest and disease problems as their larger relatives: scab, probably mildew and just possibly canker and woolly aphid might cause problems. But a small tree grown in a container is easily accessible for the application of control measures.

SUITABLE CONTAINERS
Large tubs.
HEIGHT On M.27, any variety will be limited to about 1.5m (5ft) in height, without the need for restrictive pruning. Choose M.9 for a slightly larger plant – up to 2–2.5m (6½–8ft) tall.

Malus 'Golden Hornet'

RECOMMENDED VARIETIES
'Golden Hornet', white blossom, small golden-yellow fruits; 'John Downie', white blossom, orange-red fruits (the best crab apple for culinary use); 'Profusion', purple foliage, purple blossom, small red-purple fruits; *M. tschonoskii*, pink-white flowers, small yellow brown fruit, rich orange-red autumn colour.

Prunus Ornamental cherry

> ❝ *In general, I think the ornamental cherries and their kin are highly overrated as garden plants. They suffer from disfiguring and debilitating pests and diseases, look dismal when not in flower, some of their blossom colours blend with little else, and many forms grow extremely tall and produce extensive suckers or surface roots. But despite this catalogue of woe, some among the smaller forms make good container plants.* ❞

Prunus incisa **'Kojo-no-mai'**

SPECIAL FEATURES

Avoid pruning for it will lead either to the production of suckers or to the onset of disease through pruning cuts. Remove the plants from the container when they become too large but I suggest you discard the specimen rather than plant it in the garden as mature prunus plants don't transplant well.

RECOMMENDED VARIETIES

(Heights given are after ten years). 'Amanogawa', pale pink flowers, narrow fastigiate habit, good yellow autumn colour, 4m (13ft); 'Kiku-shidare', double pink flowers, weeping habit, 3m (10ft); 'Shirotae', large double white flowers, good gold autumn colour, 4m (13ft); *P. incisa* 'Kojo-no-mai', pink-white flowers, bushy habit, 1.5–2m (5–6½ft) (the only form I have grown that has proved worthwhile for long-term container cultivation).

SUITABLE CONTAINERS

Large tubs.
HEIGHT Varies (see recommended varieties).

Prunus **'Shirotae'**

Pyrus
Ornamental pear

❝ *For reasons similar to those I put forward against crab apples (see page 82), namely, their susceptibility to pests and diseases, I am not enthusiastic about ornamental pears as garden plants. There is one exception, however, and that is* P. salicifolia *'Pendula'. Among the prettiest of weeping trees, it is easily mistaken for a willow because of its long, narrow, silvery leaves. It isn't particularly vigorous and is perfectly manageable as a container plant. Like so many weeping container trees,* P. s. *'Pendula' is undeniably seen at its best if placed in a slightly elevated position.* ❞

SPECIAL FEATURES

Although the rootstocks for pears aren't as dwarfing as those for apples, you should always choose the form called 'Quince C' for container planting. Pruning is unnecessary with P. Salicifolia 'Pendula'. It bears white flowers in mid-spring and may produce a few very hard, barely edible fruits in autumn.

SUITABLE CONTAINERS
Large tubs.
HEIGHT 4m (13ft) after ten years provided it's on 'Quince C' stock.

RECOMMENDED VARIETIES
The plant I recommend is P. salicifolia 'Pendula'. The other varieties are not really suitable for containers.

Robinia

❝ *In recent years, this more or less thorny, usually yellowish-green-leaved deciduous tree has become one of the most fashionable species to plant in small gardens. It is undeniably very pretty but it has two drawbacks, one of which is solved by planting it in a container and one of which isn't. First, it has very brittle twigs and is easily damaged by strong winds; putting it in a container enables you to reposition it in a sheltered spot. Second,* Robinia *is vigorous and isn't easily restricted by pruning, so its lifespan is limited when confined in a container.* ❞

SPECIAL FEATURES
Always position robinias so that they are generally seen with the sun behind them; the effect, in both spring and autumn, can be magical.

SUITABLE CONTAINERS
Large tubs.
HEIGHT 6m (20ft) after ten years, 12m (40ft) ultimately.

RECOMMENDED VARIETIES
Although other forms are sometimes offered, the yellow-leaved 'Frisia' is the most reliable.

Pyrus salicifolia **'Pendula'**

Sorbus

" I'm aware that in growing Sorbus in a container I have hit on something unusual. I can probably count on one hand the number of times I have seen it in a pot and I find myself asking why this should be. It is a lovely genus of medium-sized deciduous trees, some with attractive foliage, often with good autumn colours and most having beautifully coloured fruit. Most of them tolerate exposure and require little or no pruning. "

SPECIAL FEATURES

Buy sorbus in autumn when the colour of the beautiful fruits is apparent. But don't be tempted by some of the popular garden forms such as 'Joseph Rock' which really are too vigorous.

SUITABLE CONTAINERS

Large tubs.

HEIGHT 4m (13ft) after ten years (unless stated otherwise).

RECOMMENDED VARIETIES

S. aucuparia (mountain ash); 'Aspleniifolia', fern-like leaves, red-orange fruit; 'Sheerwater Seedling', typical mountain ash, red fruit, upright habit; 'Fructeo Lutea' (syn. 'Xanthocarpa') yellow fruit; *S. cashmiriana*, white fruit, 3m (10ft); *S. hupehensis*, white fruit with pink flush; *S. fruticosa*, white fruit, a low-growing shrubby plant, 2m (6½ft); *S. vilmorinii*, red to pinkish fruit, often shrubby, rather than tree-like.

Sorbus cashmiriana

Sorbus aucuparia

Dwarf or very slow-growing varieties of coniferous trees are now among the most significant and characteristic plants of the modern garden. You don't have to like them all, and I know that many people don't, but you certainly can't ignore them. Some do make very good container plants and are quite invaluable if you want to give your garden, or part of it, an Oriental feel. What follows is inevitably a very limited selection from the hundreds of dwarf conifers that exist, although many are obtainable only from specialist or selected nurseries. In the brief descriptions, my references to colour are generally to the colour in summer although some do change attractively in winter. Although deciduous conifers do exist, all those I mention here are evergreen.

Abies koreana

SPECIAL FEATURES

In the wild almost every conifer grows to tree size, but the dwarf conifers are shrubs in all but name. Occasionally, notably on prostrate varieties, wayward shoots arise and these should be cut out promptly. Otherwise pruning is not needed; a dwarf conifer is dwarf because that is the way it grows, not because it has been pruned.

SUITABLE CONTAINERS

Large tubs, although, in the short term, small tubs, window boxes and even winter hanging baskets are satisfactory for young plants.
HEIGHT Varies widely, see individual descriptions but note also the habit which is at least as important, especially in a container.

Abies Silver Fir

❝ *The silver firs are a mixed bunch, including, on the one hand, plants that are matched only by some of the spruces in their dismalness, but on the other, some with very appealing golden and silvery foliage. The genus also has the distinction of including* A. koreana, *the largest conifer that I have grown in a container. Most of the silver firs have the characteristic pyramidal 'Christmas tree' shape in overall form, but there are also some rather good prostrate forms which look very appealing when spilling over the sides of an attractive pot.* ❞

RECOMMENDED VARIETIES

A. balsamea 'Nana' (a variety called f. hudsonia is almost identical), dark green, rounded, dense habit, 30 x 30cm (12 x 12in); A. concolor 'Compacta', silvery needles, turning dark green, irregular rounded habit, 75 x 75cm (30 x 30in); A. koreana, a beautiful plant (it bears dark blue-purple cones at a younger age than any conifer I know), dark green needles with attractive silver undersides, pyramidal 1.5 x 1m (5 x 3ft) after five years and then very slowly reaches 10m (33ft); two common variants are 'Flava' with golden yellow needles and 'Silberlocke' which has twisted needles that reveal silver undersides; A. lasiocarpa 'Arizona Compacta', rich silver-blue, a densely pyramidal habit, 1m x 45cm (3ft x 18in); A. nordmanniana 'Golden Spreader' (one of my favourites but you should peg down the horizontal shoots in the early years), golden needles, at first more or less prostrate but later more rounded, 60cm x 60cm (24 x 24in); A. procera 'Glauca Prostrata', bluish-silver needles and an irregular sprawling habit, 50cm x 1.2m (20in x 4ft).

Chamaecyparis Cypress

❝ *Strictly speaking, Cupressus, with no reliable dwarf or very slow-growing forms, is the genus of true cypresses, and* Chamaecyparis *is the false. Hedges of them line mile after mile of suburbia but in dismissing them as monotonous we make two mistakes. First, we are confusing them with their close relative, the hybrid genus x* Cupressocyparis, *and, second, we assume that all cypresses must be green and dull. But, there are some fine dwarf and slow-growing forms of* Chamaecyparis *which make excellent container plants. Most are of more or less conical or domed, upright habit and possess frond-like green or yellowish shoots with no obvious needles.* ❞

RECOMMENDED VARIETIES

C. lawsoniana: 'Aurea Densa', golden yellow with a dense, rounded habit, 45 x 30cm (18 x 12in); 'Ellwood's Pillar', dark blue-green, fairly dense, markedly columnar, 75 x 30cm (30 x 12in), not to be confused with 'Ellwoodii' which is a much bigger plant; 'Gnome', blue-green, a very dense, rounded habit, 20 x 30cm (8 x 12in); 'Green Globe', bright green, a dense rounded habit, 25 x 25cm (10 x 10in); 'Minima Aurea', golden yellow, dense, more or less pyramidal, 60 x 30cm (24 x 12in); 'Pygmaea Argentea', blue-green with cream-white tips to the branches and a rounded habit, 30 x 30cm (12 x 12in); 'Silver Threads', yellow-green with yellow specks, short and stoutly columnar, 1m x 45cm (3ft x 18in). *C. obtusa* 'Nana Aurea', golden yellow, irregular spreading habit, 75 x 30cm (30 x 12in); 'Nana Gracilis', dark green, irregularly pyramidal with arching twisted branches, 1m x 60cm (3ft x 24in); 'Nana Lutea', golden yellow, irregularly pyramidal, 60 x 45cm (24 x 18in). *C. pisifera* 'Filifera Aurea', golden, slender stems and spreading, pyamidal habit, 1 x 1m (3 x 3ft); 'Nana', dark green, dense and dome-shaped.

Chamaecyparis pisifera 'Nana'

Juniperus communis 'Compressa'

Juniperus Juniper

❝ *The junipers are arguably the most valuable dwarf conifers of all. There is a wide range in habit, from very good prostrate and semi-prostrate forms to fine upright, conical varieties with green, blue-green or striking gold foliage and short, sometimes prickly needles. Container-grown dwarf junipers are the first plants that many visitors to my house see as I have a pair in terracotta pots either side of the front door. My only word of caution: some junipers will not remain dwarf. Five or six years may be the effective container lifespan for some spreading varieties.* ❞

RECOMMENDED VARIETIES

J. communis: 'Compressa', blue-green, dense and neatly columnar, 1.5m x 30cm (5ft x 12in); 'Depressa Aurea', golden yellow in summer but turning more green in winter, prostrate, 50cm x 1.5m (20in x 5ft); 'Green Carpet', dense, greenish-bronze, prostrate, 15cm x 1m (6in x 3ft). *J. horizonalis*: 'Blue Chip', bluish-green with feathery shoots, prostrate, 30cm x 1.5m (12in x 5ft); 'Emerald Spreader', bright green, prostrate, 15cm x 2m (6in x 6½ft); 'Prince of Wales', bright green, 15cm x 1m (6in x 3ft). *J. procumbens*: 'Nana', bright green, prostrate, 25cm x 1.5m (10in x 5ft); *J. recurva* 'Densa', bright green, semi-prostrate, 40cm x 1m (16in x 3ft); *J. sabina* 'Tamariscifolia', bluish-green, prostrate, 45cm x 1.5m (18in x 5ft).

Picea Spruce

❝ *The genus* Picea *can boast a species that probably outnumbers every other conifer that is grown in a container, but it is still not on my recommended list.* Picea *is the spruce genus and one of its species,* P. abies, *the Norway spruce, is still the most popular Christmas tree. Many people keep them from year to year, either in the container or in the open garden, but this is not a reliable operation and nor is the plant worth the effort. Elsewhere in the genus there are rather attractive dwarf trees, generally with a pyramidal shape and short, prickly needles and a range of shades through blue, green and yellow.* ❞

RECOMMENDED VARIETIES

P. abies: 'Inversa', dark green, prostrate, 20cm x 1.5m (8in x 5ft); 'Little Gem', bright green, compact, upright, 30 x 30cm (12 x 12in); 'Pygmaea', dark green, broadly pyramidal, 30 x 20cm (12 x 8in).
P. glauca: P. g. albertiana 'Alberta Globe', bright green and dome-shaped, 30 x 45cm (12 x 18in); 'Conica', bright green and cone shaped, 1m x 60cm (3ft x 24in); 'Laurin', 30 x 15cm (12 x 6in). P. mariana: 'Ericoides', rounded, compact, spreading, 45cm x 1m (18in x 3ft); 'Nana', bluish-green and rounded, 15 x 25cm (6 x 10in). P. omorika: 'Nana', dark green, silvery beneath, rounded, but soon outgrows its space, 1.5m x 75cm (5ft x 30in). P. pungens: 'Globosa', steely-blue with an irregularly rounded habit, 60 x 60cm (24 x 24in); 'Hoopsii', truly steel-blue, broadly conical, 2.5m x 1.2m (8ft x 4ft); 'Procumbens', steel-blue, semi-prostrate, 30cm x 50cm (12in x 20in).

Picea abies 'Little Gem'

Pinus Pine

❝ *For some curious reason, many gardeners seem to forget the pines when selecting dwarf conifers. This is a great shame, for the genus includes some of the loveliest and most striking plants, and many that make excellent subjects for growing in containers. They are distinguished most readily from other conifers by their long, sometimes very long, fairly soft needles and they mainly adopt a more or less pyramidal shape with a range of green, bluish and yellow shades. Some of my most effective container plantings have included at least one dwarf pine and I hope yours will too.* ❞

RECOMMENDED VARIETIES

The groups within the genus are distinguished by the numbers of needles in each leaf cluster.
Two-needled pines: P. contorta 'Frisian Gold', golden yellow and irregularly rounded, 60 x 60cm (24 x 24in); P. heldreichii leucodermis 'Schmidtii', dark green, irregularly rounded, 40 x 40cm (16 x 16in); P. mugo 'Mops', bright green, irregularly rounded, 75 x 75cm (30 x 30in); P. sylvestris 'Doone Valley', greenish silver, irregularly rounded, 45 x 45cm (18 x 18in).
Five-needled pines: P. strobus 'Reinshaus', bluish-green, irregularly rounded, a delightful plant that always arouses comment in my garden, people want to stroke it, 75 x 75cm (30 x 30in).

Taxus Yew

The yew occupies a special place in gardening for many reasons: there is no other evergreen that matches its dense foliage and neat compact habit; nothing clips better; there is no finer species for topiary; and no plant, conifer or otherwise makes a better hedge. None of this necessarily means it is an ideal subject for a container but, if you do want movable topiary, yew certainly supplies the wherewithall. In addition, there are a few dwarf varieties worthy of a place in any container, and one golden variety makes a magnificent feature, however it is grown.

Pinus leucodermis 'Schmidtii'

Taxus baccata

Thuja occidentalis 'Danica'

Thuja Red Cedar

Much less well known as hedging plants than they should be, the thujas, or red cedars, are fine, soft-foliaged, rather pleasantly scented conifers. They include some truly beautiful dwarf and slow-growing forms. I have more thujas in my garden than any other conifer except yew, partly by virtue of having a windbreak composed of them, but also because I simply adore them as container plants. One word of caution: I and some other people develop a slight skin rash after handling the foliage.

HERBS

Herbs seem almost designed to be grown in containers, combining, as they do, attractiveness with function. They need to be close to the kitchen, and this may mean they are kept some distance from the kitchen garden or indeed from open soil beds of any sort. Whether your garden is near or far, I do think a small collection of herbs in attractive terracotta pots is a must for everyone.

Allium sativum Garlic

❝ Garlic, I expect you will say, is an annual garden vegetable and no more appropriate than onions for container cultivation. But if you think of it in the same way as chives and grow it for its foliage to cut into salads, you will be pleasantly surprised. The splendid characteristic garlic flavour is there, but in rather milder form. Garlic is a true perennial, and can be maintained for year after year in a pot. All you have to do is divide it every two or three years. ❞

SPECIAL FEATURES
Garlic sometimes produces pinkish flowers, but generally the flower buds abort and form stem-tip bulbils instead.

SUITABLE CONTAINERS
Small pots, window boxes.
HEIGHT Normally attains about 30cm (12in).

RECOMMENDED VARIETIES
I don't know of any selected forms of *Allium sativum* but you may come across the variety *A. s. ophioscorodon* which has twisted stems. This variety is sometimes called 'rocambole' although that name is more generally used for a related species, *A. scorodoprasum*. This is the giant garlic, a huge plant that would be a serious embarrassment in a container.

Allium schoeno-prasum Chives

❝ Chive is the best known of the herb onions, and probably the prettiest too. It would be well worth growing for its mauve or white flowers alone and it is equally valuable as a culinary herb and as a container plant. ❞

SPECIAL FEATURES
Chives can be raised from seed but in my experience, this never produces the best plants; you are well advised to buy a plant and divide it annually. Chives are fairly vigorous and will produce a reasonably large clump within a year. Encourage the foliage by cutting off the flower stalks, although the flowers are edible too. It is likely to suffer from rust.

SUITABLE CONTAINERS
Small pots, window boxes.
HEIGHT Generally attains around 25cm (10in) although some named forms may be twice as tall.

RECOMMENDED VARIETIES
The normal, mauve-flowered species is very pretty but, if you have room, combine it with the larger pink 'Forescate'; the dwarf and strangely twisted 'Shepherd's Crooks'; the white-flowered variant, usually called simply 'White'.

Chives, parsley and other herbs bring life to old plant pots

Laurus nobilis Bay

❝ *You will inevitably grow more bay than you ever need, since it is potentially a rather large evergreen shrub and yet only a leaf or two is used at a time. But bay is a versatile container plant and, probably, the herb is grown more often for its ornamental rather than culinary value. You can pay handsomely for clipped specimens in pretty pots, but it is perfectly easy and very rewarding to buy a rooted cutting and produce your own.* ❞

SPECIAL FEATURES
Moderately hardy, but likely to be browned or defoliated by cold winter winds, although it will almost always regenerate from old wood.

SUITABLE CONTAINERS
Small pots, window boxes, large tubs (for large clipped specimens).
HEIGHT Left to its own devices, bay forms a tree 12m (40ft) tall but it can be readily clipped to limit these ambitions. A small plant shouldn't grow more than about 15cm (6in) in a season.

RECOMMENDED VARIETIES
The normal species, *Laurus nobilis*, is the only one in the genus worth growing for its culinary and ornamental appeal. The golden form, 'Aurea', is an anaemic-looking thing.

Laurus nobilis

Ocimum basilicum Basil

❝ *If you enjoy tomato salad, then you must enjoy basil because the two are inseparable. Growing basil does require a little more work than some herbs; although a short-lived perennial, it is always grown as an annual and so must be raised afresh each season from seed. But this is an easy task and, by raising your own basil, you can enjoy not only the plain green-leaved form but also some of the rather pretty variants.* ❞

SPECIAL FEATURES
The seed will germinate easily if it is lightly covered, but remember that none of the varieties are hardy. They should be brought under cover or sown afresh in the autumn for indoor cultivation over winter.

SUITABLE CONTAINERS
Small pots, window boxes.
HEIGHT Varies with variety but most attain about 25cm (10in).

RECOMMENDED VARIETIES
The normal species, *Ocimum basilicum*, from tropical Asia has broad, bright green, freshly scented leaves; *O. purpurascens* has red-purple leaves and a spicy fragrance; *O. citriodorum* is lemon-scented; *O.* 'Cinnamon', spicy; *O. minimum*, the so-called Greek basil, has smaller leaves and is a neat, bushy plant, pretty but not as well flavoured.

Ocimum basilicum

Mentha spp. Mint

❝ *Mint is one of those plants I always grow in a container, even if the container is sunk into the soil of my herb bed. Without a doubt mint is the most invasive of herbs and, left to its own devices, it will very soon take over a plot. Even when it (or, more correctly, they, as there are several choice varieties) is grown more conventionally as a container plant, don't put other herbs in the same pot if you want them to have a fighting chance of survival.* ❞

SPECIAL FEATURES

Grow mints in containers for year-round use by all means, and repot them at least every two years because of their vigorous growth. But, if you already have an established herb garden, pot up a few mint runners in the late autumn and bring them into the house or greenhouse; this way you will get fresh green shoots several weeks earlier in the new season.

SUITABLE CONTAINERS

Small pots, window boxes (but only confined within individual pots).
HEIGHT The forms that I recommend here for growing in containers shouldn't exceed about 60cm (24in) tall.

RECOMMENDED VARIETIES

Mentha spicata, spearmint (the best for new potatoes); *M. suaveolens*, applemint (the best for mint sauces); *M. x piperita*, peppermint; *citrata*, eau de cologne mint (exquisite fragrance); *M. x gracilis* 'Variegata', ginger mint.

Mentha spicata

'Curled' parsley

Petroselinum crispum Parsley

❝ *The shame about parsley is that it is too often used solely as a garnish and left on people's plates. Yet it is the most versatile and freshest-tasting of herbs, invaluable in the kitchen in so many ways and invaluable, too, for taking the smell of onion or garlic from the breath. It is, I think, unique among herbs in having a particular type of container named after it, the many-holed parsley pot.* ❞

SPECIAL FEATURES

Like many of its relatives, parsley is a biennial, but in pots it really must be grown as an annual; it becomes much less tasty when it produces flower heads in the second year. Try to grow it from seed, adding a little lime to the compost if germination is stubborn; but if all else fails, buy a few plants.

SUITABLE CONTAINERS

Small pots (including parsley pots), window boxes.
HEIGHT The compact varieties attain around 20cm (8in), the taller types up to 60cm (24in) in leaf, and taller still in flower.

RECOMMENDED VARIETIES

The neatest and prettiest types of parsley for containers are the 'Moss' or 'Curled' varieties. If you want to grow a taller one, choose Italian parsley (*neapolitanum*) which has the finest flavour of all.

Rosmarinus officinalis Rosemary

❝ Rosemary is in the same league as bay (see page 91): it's a very big shrubby plant but you need only a small amount in the kitchen. You couldn't quite describe it as ornamental, however, although it does make a good hedge. Nonetheless, a small, neatly clipped plant can be most attractive in a container and I have even seen rosemary in an ornamental pot used as a subject for topiary. ❞

SPECIAL FEATURES
If you can provide shelter in winter, you have the option of growing some of the rather less hardy and very ornamental forms, although none surpass the normal species for flavour.

SUITABLE CONTAINERS
Large tubs, small tubs, window boxes (if renewed at least every two years from cuttings).
HEIGHT The taller varieties can reach up to 2m (6½ft) but all can be limited by clipping, which should be started at an early age.

RECOMMENDED VARIETIES
The normal pale blue-flowered form is widely obtainable, but look out for other flower colours and for dwarf variants; 'Lockwood Variety', low-growing, dark blue flowers; 'Tuscan Blue', dark blue flowers; 'Majorca Pink', pink flowers.

Salvia spp. Sage

❝ Sage has a reputation for being a nuisance: it is a useful culinary herb but not always the most attractive and, for some reason, there is a myth that the ornamental-leaved forms aren't edible. With a range of sages you can achieve a very pretty container planting. ❞

SPECIAL FEATURES
A sage plant in flower is no beauty, so cut back the stems promptly. Renew the plants from cuttings every two years.

SUITABLE CONTAINERS
Small pots, window boxes.
HEIGHT Most of the best forms attain about 40–50cm (16–20in).

RECOMMENDED VARIETIES
'Icterina', pale green leaves with a gold variegation; 'Purpurascens', deep-purple leaves; 'Purpurascens Variegata', deep-purple leaves with angular cream and pink blotches; 'Tricolor', pale green leaves with a white and pink variegated pattern.

Thymus spp. Thyme

❝ It is easy to make a mistake and end up with a thyme that is neither of culinary use nor ornamental, when it should be both. I have limited my selection to those I have found valuable in both respects. ❞

SPECIAL FEATURES
Bushy types soon become woody and straggly, and should be renewed every two years. The best culinary forms don't come true from seed.

SUITABLE CONTAINERS
Small pots, window boxes.
HEIGHT Varies from about 5cm (2in) to about 20cm (8in).

RECOMMENDED VARIETIES
T. pseudolanuginosus, pink flowers, very woolly leaves; *T. pulegioides*, large leaves; *T. vulgaris* 'Silver Posie', neat, bushy, silver variegation, the best of all for flavour.

Thymus 'Silver Posie'

Salvia officinalis 'Tricolor'

INDEX

Page numbers in *italic* refer to illustrations.

A
Abies 86
　A. balsamea 86
　A. concolor 86
　A. koreana 86, *86*
　A. lasiocarpa 86
　A. nordmanniana 86
　A. procera 86
Acer 80
　A. japonicum 80
　A. japonicum 'Aureum' *81*
　A. palmatum 80, *80*
　A. p. atropurpureum 80
　A. p. dissectum 80
　A. shirasawanum 80
Agapanthus 60
　A. 'Headbourne Hybrids'
　　60
Ageratum 18
　'Capri' *18*
Ajuga 52
　A. reptans 52
　'Braunherz' *52*
Allium 60
　A. beesianum 60
　A. cyathophorum farreri 60
　A. flavum 60
　A. karataviense 60
　A. moly 60
　A. oreophilum 60
　A. sativum 90
　A. s. ophioscorodon 90
　A. schoenoprasum 90
　A. scorodoprasum 90
Alopecurus pratensis 55
Alyssum 18
Amelanchier 81
　A. canadensis 81
　A. lamarckii 81, *81*
Anchusa 19
　'Blue Angel' *19*
Anemone 61
　A. blanda 61
　A. coronaria 61
　'De Caen' *61*
　A. nemorosa 61
Argyranthemum 44
Artemisia 52
　A. absinthium 'Lambrook
　　Silver' *52*, *52*
　A. arborescens 52
　A. stelleriana 52
Asplenium 55
　A. scolopendrium 54
Aster 19
　'Milady Mixed' *19*
Aucuba 71
　A. japonica 71
　'Picturata' *71*

B
barrels 8, *8*
Basil see *Ocimum basilicum*

Bay see *Laurus nobilis*
Begonia 20, 44
　B. masoniana 44
　B. rex 44
　B. semperflorens 9, 20
　'Olympian White'
　　20
　B. sutherlandii 44, *44*
　B. x tuberhybrida 44
Bellflower see *Campanula*
Bellis 20
　B. perennis 20
Bergenia 53
　B. cordifolia 53
Bindweed see *Convolvulus*
Box see *Buxus*
Brachyscome 21
　'Blue Star' *21*
Briza maxima 29, *29*
　B. media 29
Broom see *Cytisus*
Browallia 21
　'Blue Troll' *21*
Buddleja 71
　B. alternifolia 71
　B. davidii 71
　B. fallowiana alba 71
　B. x lewisiana 'Margaret
　　Pike' 71
Bugle see *Ajuga*
bulbs 12, 60-68
Busy Lizzie see *Impatiens*
Butterfly flower see
　Schizanthus
Buxus 72
　B. sempervirens 72
　'Suffruticosa' *72*

C
Calceolaria 22, *22*
Calendula 22, *22*
Californian bluebell see
　Nemophila
Callistephus chinensis 19
Camellia 72
　C. x williamsii 72
　'Donation' *72*
Campanula 23
　C. isophylla 23
　'Kristal Hybrids' *23*
Cedar, red see *Thuja*
Cerastium tomentosum 23,
　23
Chamaecyparis 87
　C. lawsoniana 87
　C. obtusa 87
　C. pisifera 87
　'Nana' *87*
Cherry pie see
　Heliotropium
Chives see *Allium
　schoenoprasum*
Choisya 71
Chrysanthemum 24, 53
　'Pennine Jewel' *53*
　'Wessex Wine' *53*

C. coronarium 24
　'Golden Gem' 24, *24*
C. multicaule 24
C. paludosum 24
Cineraria 24
　C. maritima 24, *24*
Clematis 73
　C. macropetala 'Maidwell
　　Hall' *73*
　C. montana 73
coir 10
Coleus 25, *25*
composts 5, 10
conifers, dwarf 86-89
containers
　benefits 5
　constraints 5
　lead 14, *14*
　plastic 7
　stability 6
　stone 8
　terracotta 7
　types 4, 6-9
　wooden 8, 9
Convolvulus 25
　C. mauritanicus 25, *25*
　C. tricolor 25
Coreopsis 26
　C. basalis 26
　C. tinctoria 26, *26*
Cortaderia selloana 55
Crab apple see *Malus*
Crocus 61
Cuphea 26
　C. hyssopifolia 26
　C. ignea 26, *26*
Cupressus 87
Cyclamen 62
　C. coum 62, *62*
　C. hederifolium 62
　C. persicum 62
Cypress see
　Chamaecyparis
Cytisus 73
　C. battandieri 73
　C. x beanii 73
　C. x kewensis 73

D
Daffodils 65
Dead-nettles see *Lamium*
deadheading 13
Dendranthema 53
design 14-16
Dianthus 27
　'Strawberry Parfait' *27*
Diascia 27
doors, front 16, *16*
dwarf conifers 86-89

E
Eccremocarpus 28
　E. scaber 28, *28*
Elymus magellanicus 55
Erigeron 28
　E. karvinskianus 28, *28*

F
Fatsia 74
　F. japonica 'Variegata' *74*
feeding 13
Ferns 54
fertilizers 13
Festuca glauca 55, *55*
floribunda roses 70
Floss flower see *Ageratum*
foliar feeding 13
free-standing containers 6
front doors 16, *16*
fruit 17
Fuchsia 4, 45-46
　'Annabel' *45*
　standards 46
　'Tennessee Waltz' *45*

G
Galanthus 62
　G. atkinsii 62
　G. nivalis 62
garden design 14-16
Garlic see *Allium sativum*
Gazania 29
　'Daybreak' *29*
Geranium 54
　G. cinereum 54
　G. c. subcaulescens 54
　G. dalmaticum 54, *55*
　G. himalayense 54
　G. x lindavicum 54
　G. x oxonianum 54
　G. phaeum 54
　G. procurrens 54
　G. pylzowianum 54
　G. x riversleaianum 54
　G. sanguineum 54
　G. s. lancastriense 54
Gerbera 47
　G. jamesonii 47
Glechoma hederacea 48
Grasses 29, 55
growing-bags 9

H
Hakonechloa macra 55
half-barrels 8, *8*
Hamamelis 74
　H. mollis 74, *74*
　H. x intermedia 74
hanging baskets 4, 9, 11
　planting 11
hard surfaces 15
hardy perennials 52-59
Hedera 56
　H. helix 56, *56*
Helichrysum 4, 47
　H. microphyllum 47
　H. petiolare 47, *47*
Helictotrichon sempervirens
　55
Heliotropium 30
　'Marina Purple Splendour'
　　30
Helleborus 56

H. argutifolius 56
H. foetidus 56
H. niger 56
H. orientalis 56
herbs 17, 90-93
Holcus mollis 55
Hordeum jubatum 29
Hosta 57
　H. albopicta 57
　H. aurea marginata 56
　H. crispula 57
　H. fortunei 57
　H. lancifolia 57
　H. sieboldiana 57, *57*
　H. undulata albomarginata
　　57
Hyacinth see *Hyacinthus*
Hyacinthus 63
　'Ostara' *63*
　H. orientalis 63
hybrid tea roses 70
Hydrangea 5, 75
　'Madame Emile Mouilliere'
　　75
　H. aspera 75
　H. involucrata 75
　H. macrophylla 75
　H. paniculata 75
　H. serrata 75
　H. villosa 75

I
Impatiens 30
　'Blitz' *30*
Iris 10, 63
　I. danfordiae 63
　I. reticulata 63
　I. unguicularis 63
Ivy see *Hedera*

J
Jekyll, Gertrude 28
John Innes composts 10
Juniper see *Juniperus*
Juniperus 87
　J. communis 87
　'Compressa' *87*
　J. horizontalis 87
　J. procumbens 87
　J. recurva 87
　J. sabina 87

L
Lagurus ovatus 29
Lamium 57
　L. galeobdolon 57
　L. maculatum 57
Lantana 48
　L. camara 48, *48*
　L. montevidensis 48
Lathyrus 31
　'Patio Mixed' *31*
Laurus nobilis 91, *91*
Lavandula 76
　L. angustifolia 76
　L. x intermedia 76

L. stoechas 76, *76*
Lavender see *Lavandula*
lead containers 14, *14*
Lilium 64
  'Bright Star' *64*
  L. candidum 64
  L. hansonii 64
  L. henryi 64
  L. martagon 64
  L. monadelphum 64
  L. regale 64
  L. speciosum 64
Lily see *Lilium*
Lobelia 9, 31
  'Riviera Lilac' *31*
Lobularia maritima 18
long-term plants 13
Lysimachia 58
  L. nummularia 58
    'Aurea' *58*

M
Magnolia 82
  M. liliiflora 82, *82*
  M. x loebneri 82
  M. x soulangeana 82
  M. x stellata 82
Malus 82
  'Golden Hornet' *82*
  M. tschonoskii 82
Marigold see *Tagetes*
materials 7
Matricaria 32
  'Snow Dwarf' *32*
Matthiola 32
  'Brompton Stock' *32*
Mentha 92
  M. citrata 92
  M. x gracilis 92
  M. x piperita 92
  M. spicata 92, *92*
  M. suaveolens 92
Mimulus 33
  'Malibu' series *33*
Mint see *Mentha*
Mock orange see *Philadelphus*
Molinia caerulea 55
mulching 13

N
Narcissus 65
  'Tête-a-Tête' *64*
  N. asturiensis 65
  N. bulbocodium conspicuus 65
  N. poeticus recurvus 65
  N. pseudonarcissus 65
  N. tazeta lacticolor 65
Nasturtium see *Tropaeolum*
Nemesia 33
  'Carnival' *33*
Nemophila 34
  'Baby Blue Eyes' *34*
  N. menziesii 34
Nepeta 48
Nerine 66

N. bowdenii 66, *66*
Nicotiana 34
  'Domino Salmon Pink' *34*
Nierembergia 35
  N. repens 35
Nolana 35
  N. paradoxa 'Blue Bird' 35, *35*

O
Ocimum basilicum 91, *91*
  O. citriodorum 91
  O. minimum 91
  O. purpurascens 91
Ornamental cherry see *Prunus*
Ornamental pear see *Pyrus*
Osteospermum 35
  'Glistening White' *35*

P
Pansy *5*, 43
Parsley see *Petroselinum crispum*
Passiflora 49
  P. antioquiensis 49, *49*
  P. caerulea 49
  P. x caeruleoracemosa 49
  P. edulis 49
  P. exoniensis 49
  P. mollissima 49
  P. quadrangularis 49
Passion flower see *Passiflora*
peat 10
Pelargonium 16, 36-37
  'Dolly Varden' *37*
  'Lord Bute' *37*
  'Multibloom Salmon' *36*
  'Summer Showers' *37*
perennials
  hardy 52-59
  tender 44-51
Periwinkle see *Vinca*
Petroselinum crispum 92
Petunia 38-39
  'Birthday Celebration' *38*
  'Mirage Sugar' *38*
Philadelphus 77
  'Beauclerk' *77*
  'Belle Etoile' *77*
Picea 88
P. abies 88
  'Little Gem' *88*
  P. glauca 88
  P. g. albertiana 88
  P. mariana 88
  P. omorika 88
  P. pungens 88
Pine see *Pinus*
Pinus 88
  P. contorta 88
  P. heldreichii leucodermis 88
  P. leucodermis 'Schmidtii' 89
  P. mugo 88
  P. strobus 88
  P. sylvestris 88
planting 11-12

plastic containers 7
Plecostachys serpyllifolia 47
Plectranthus 49
  P. australis 49
  P. forsteri 'Marginatus' 49
  P. madagascariensis 49
  P. oertendahlii 49, *49*
Polypodium vulgare 54
Polystichum setiferum 54
Poor man's orchid see *Schizanthus*
Pot marigold see *Calendula*
Potatoes 17
Potentilla 76
  P. fruticosa 76
  'Primrose Beauty' *76*
Primula 58
  P. juliae 58
  P. vulgaris 58, *58*
pruning 13
Prunus 83
  'Shirotae' *83*
  P. incisa 'Kojo-no-mai' 83, *83*
Pyrus 84
  P. salicifolia 'Pendula' 84, *84*

R
Red cedar see *Thuja*
repotting 13
Rhodochiton 50
  R. atrosanguineum 50, *50*
Rhododendron 78
  'Razorbill' *78*
  R. impeditum 78
  R. pemakoense 78
  R. williamsianum 78
  R. yakushimanum 78
Robinia 84
Rosa 69-70
  'Fritz Nobis' *70*
  'Nozomi' *70*
  'Tear Drop' *69*
  'The Fairy' *70*
Rosemary see *Rosmarinus officinalis*
Roses see *Rosa*
Rosmarinus officinalis 93

S
Sage see *Salvia*
Salpiglossis 39
  'Festival' *39*
Salvia 40, 93
  'Red Rivers' *40*
  S. officinalis 'Tricolor' *93*
  S. splendens 40
Scaevola 50
  S. aemula 50
  'Blue Fan' *51*
Schizanthus 40
  'Dwarf Bouquet' *40*
Scilla 66
  S. mischtschenkoana 66, *67*
  S. siberica 66

Senecio 22
  S. cineraria 24
shrubs 71-79
Silver fir see *Abies*
Snow-in-summer see *Cerastium tomentosum*
Snowdrop see *Galanthus*
soil-based composts 10
soil-free composts 10
Sorbus 85
  S. aucuparia 85, *85*
  S. cashmiriana 85, *85*
  S. fruticosa 85
  S. hupehensis 85
  S. vilmorinii 85
Spruce see *Picea*
standard fuchsias 46
standard roses 70
Stars of the Veldt see *Osteospermum*
steps, containers on 16, *16*
Stipa arundinacea 55
  S. gigantea 55
stone containers 8
strawberry pots, planting 12
summer plants 12, 13
surfaces, hard 15
Swan River daisy see *Brachyscome*
Swedish ivy see *Plectranthus*
Sweet pea see *Lathyrus*

T
Tagetes 41
  'Golden Gem' *41*
  T. erecta 41
  T. patula 41
Taxus 89
  T. baccata 89, *89*
tender perennials 13, 44-51
terracotta containers 7
Thuja 89
  T. occidentalis 89
  'Danica' 89, *89*
  T. orientalis 89
  T. plicata 89
Thunbergia 41
  T. alata 41
Thyme see *Thymus*
Thymus 17, 93
  'Silver Posie' *93*
  T. pseudolanuginosus 93
  T. pulegioides 93
  T. vulgaris 93
Tomatoes 13
topiary 16, *16*
Tradescantia 51
  T. x andersoniana 51
  T. fluminensis 51
  T. zebrina 51, *51*
trees 80-85
Tropaeolum 42
  T. majus 42
  T. peregrinum 42, *42*
tubs 4
  planting 12

Tulipa 67
  'Angelique' *67*
  'Red Riding Hood' *67*
  'Spring Green' *7*
  T. acuminata 68
  T. biflora 68
  T. clusiana 68
  T. humilus 68
  T. kaufmanniana 68
  T. kolpakowskiana 68
  T. linifolia 68
  T. orphanidia 68
  T. praestans 68
  T. saxatilis 68
  T. sprengeri 68
  T. sylvestris 68
  T. tarda 68
  T. turkestanica 68
  T. urumiensis 68

V
vegetables 17, *17*
Verbena 42
  'Loveliness' *38*
  'Sissinghurst' *43*
Viburnum 79
  V. x burkwoodii 79
  V. x carlcephalum 79, *79*
  V. carlesii 79
  V. davidii 79, *79*
Vinca 59
  V. minor 59
Viola 43
  'Universal' *43*

W
watering *5*, 13
window boxes 4, *4*, 9, *9*
  planting 12
winter plants 12
Witch hazel see *Hamamelis*
wooden containers 8, 9

Y
Yew see *Taxus*
Yucca 59
  Y. filamentosa 59
  Y. flaccida 59
  Y. glauca 59
  Y. gloriosa 59
    'Variegata' *59*
  Y. recurvifolia 59

Z
Zantedeschia 68

PHOTOGRAPHIC ACKNOWLEDGMENTS

Professor Stefan Buczacki 41, 64 top;

Anthony Cooper 21 top;

Eric Crichton 7 bottom left, 9 top, 9 bottom, 14 left, 28 left, 33 bottom, 37 left, 55 centre left, 58 right, 67 top right, 67 bottom, 81 left, 87 right, 92 left;

John Fielding 12 bottom right, 19 top, 52 right, 62, 76 top, 93 left;

Garden Picture Library /Sunniva Harte 83 bottom, /Marie O'Hara front cover bottom left, /Brigitte Thomas 38 right;

John Glover 2 top left, 7 top right, 14 right, 16 left, 16 right, 17 left, 17 right, 21 bottom, 49 bottom, 57 right, 75, 82 top, 86, 93 right;

Harpur Garden Library 85 bottom;

Andrew Lawson Back Cover, 2-3 background, 4 left, 20 left, 22 bottom, 35 right, 37 right, 40 top, 43 top, 50, 58, 69, 70 right, 89 left;

Clive Nichols Photography 4 right, 5 right, 6, 7 bottom right, 10, 11, 47 right, 56, 60 right, 64 bottom, 70 top left, 85 top;

Octopus Publishing Group Ltd./Paul Barker 5 left, /Jerry Harpur 81 right, /Andrew Lawson front cover background and bottom right, 1 top, 77 left, /Steve Wooster 1 bottom, 8, 15, 57 left, /George Wright 33 top;

Photos Horticultural 12 top left, 18, 19 bottom, 20 right, 22 top, 23 top, 25 bottom, 27, 29 left, 30 top right, 34 top, 35 left, 36, 37 centre, 38 left, 44, 47 left, 51 top, 51 bottom, 52 left, 53 right, 55 top left, 55 bottom right, 60 left, 61, 71, 72 right, 74 bottom, 76 bottom, 77 right, 78, 79 bottom, 82 bottom, 83 top, 84, 88, 89 top right, 90, 91 right;

Harry Smith Collection 23 bottom, 24 left, 24 right, 25 top, 26 top, 26 bottom, 28 right, 29 right, 30 bottom left, 31 top, 31 bottom, 32 left, 32 right, 34 bottom, 39, 40 bottom, 42, 43 bottom, 45 top left, 45 top right, 45 bottom, 48, 49 top, 53 left, 55 bottom left, 59, 63, 66, 67 top left, 70 bottom left, 72 left, 73, 74 top, 79 top, 80, 87 left, 89 bottom right, 91 left, 92 right

Acuba